BREWERS LOOP

BREWERS LOOP

BETH & STEVE PIPE

A Loopy tour of
Lake District breweries

First published in 2023
by Palatine Books,
Carnegie House,
Chatsworth Road
Lancaster LA1 4SL
www.palatinebooks.com

British Library Cataloguing-in-Publication data
A catalogue record for this book is available from the British Library

Paperback ISBN 13: 978-1-910837-45-0

Designed and typeset by Carnegie Book Production
www.carnegiebookproduction.com

Printed and bound by Micropress

For Andy, who always made us smile

Contents

Preface   xi
Prologue   xix
Another fine mess   1
Full steam ahead   13
Row, row, row your boat   25
Tour de Windermere   37
An uphill struggle   49
Water ridiculous idea   59
Up   69
Best boot forwards!   83
Oohhh matron!   97
Life of a 'Life of a Mountain' bloke   111
Rescue me   123
I wandered lonely as a beer cask   135
Sister act   147
We are family   159
Buzzing!   173
La'al rascal   185
Raining it in   195
Final flocking day   205
Epilogue part I   217
Epilogue part II   219
Epilogue part III – son of epilogue   221
Epilogue part IV – daughter of epilogue – summer '21 223

Preface

'It'll test any marriage'

WHEN I TOOK OFF on the hike for *Gin, Cake and Rucksacks* with a virtual stranger, several reviewers and interviewers commented that it was a hike which would 'test any marriage', well, challenge accepted.

Me and Steve (or should that be Steve and I? If I'm serious about this book writing malarkey I really should figure that one out!) have been on some pretty impressive adventures together, including living in our campervan (Delores) for three months, in the middle of winter, because we couldn't find a house when we first moved up here.

We hadn't been on many multi-day hikes together though, could that be a problem? I did what all sensible folks do when they have a question like that; I asked the internet.

'When out hiking with your partner, have you ever had a difference of opinion over something pertaining to the hike?' I asked. The internet said yes they had. Well, 87 per cent of them said yes and I reckon the other 13 per cent are lying through their teeth.

I'd definitely missed Steve on the gin hike, so the idea of making this a joint venture appealed, the problem now was that we needed a responsible adult around to help us with the planning and to step in when conversations like this began to spiral out of control.

'We need to plot a route visiting all the microbreweries.'

'We should make it more interesting.'

'Interesting how?'

'We should carry a barrel with us or something.'

'Great idea, and we could take it up a mountain!'

'Brilliant – and how about canoeing with it?'

'Cycling with it!'

'Swimming with it!'

Neither of us can quite remember who had which ridiculous idea. When everything was going well, of course, we both wanted to claim it was us that had the genius idea of, say, canoeing along Windermere, but when we were actually canoeing along Windermere, directly into a full-on head wind, it was clearly the other idiot's brainwave, and we never should have listened to them in the first place.

What are we really like? Well, I'm loud, impulsive and a bit of a control freak (personally I prefer the term 'very well organised'), whereas Steve is quieter, much better at thinking things through before making rash decisions and, although he always means to put things back where they came from, he very rarely does.

Are we big drinkers? Well, me more so than Steve to be fair. Steve prefers lighter, golden ales, whereas I'll drink pretty much anything. I blame my genes. Below is a photo of my maternal granddad – he and my nan owned a bar for many years and, for many more years after that, he worked as a bar man. In fact, beer was one of the very first smells I remember; I can clearly recall him giving me a bristly kiss and the smell of beer on his breath and clothes. He was known for his fondness of a pint and there are several entertaining family stories on the subject, including the fact that my nan painted two large white stripes on the entry to the ginnel leading to their house so he could always find his way home.

Ahead of us lay eighteen days of tough hiking in, what turned out to be, one of the hottest summers on record, hauling 24 kilos of beer cask and trolley, as well as our huge Berghaus backpacks. Oh, and, it turns out, I forgot to add in any rest days. What could possibly go wrong?

Beth's grandfather, beer man and champion gurner

After all that, we barely skipped a beat when we were out hiking; sure we had the odd grumpy moment or two, who wouldn't? It turns out that actually sitting down and writing the book together was by far the bigger challenge. Usually, when we work together, I do the words and he does the pictures and there's not a lot of overlap, but this time we had to write the words together, and that's where the trouble started. I'm very much a 'plan ahead and get it all done way before the deadline' kind of a gal, whereas he's much more of a 'slide over the finish line as the last second is ticking down before the deadline' bloke. To be fair, I already knew that, I'd just somehow convinced myself that this would be different. I was wrong. Still, we mopped most of the blood off the manuscript before we handed it in ...

Mountain Rescue

Having decided on a ridiculous adventure we thought it would be rather nice to raise some money for a good cause along the way, and who better than Mountain Rescue? We have never had need of their services thus far (to be fair, it's been a close call on a few occasions), and although they are a vital emergency service they are entirely funded by donations and staffed by volunteers.

Given that we were about to embark on such a ridiculous mission, it seemed only right that they should benefit in some small way. Call it hedging our bets. All told we raised just over £1000 for them on the hike itself, and will be donating 10 per cent of the profits of this book to them too.

A great big THANK YOU

We both want to say a HUGE thank you to a few folks before we get stuck into the book. First up is Unsworth's Brewery who, when we first had the slightly deranged idea of dragging an empty beer cask around the county, immediately identified cask #056 as being the perfect cask for the task. They were right. They also didn't bat an eyelid when the plans evolved and it became apparent that we were going to plaster the cask with stickers and subject it to a range of non-beer related activities. We retuned #056 to them at the end of the hike and he (yes, we bonded) continues to live there, enjoying a happy retirement, on display in their tap room. If you visit, tell him we said 'hi'.

The cask at the start of our journey

We also owe an immense debt of gratitude to Hesket Newmarket brewery who loaned us the trolley which, as I type, is still living in our garage and really does need to be returned to them. We visited them a couple of weeks before the hike, still with no clear idea of how we would transport the cask around the county, and they stepped in with the offer of a trolley and an assurance that we wouldn't be able to break it. Quite simply we could not have completed the hike without the trolley. It was a godsend. We abused it dreadfully, especially on the Helvellyn day, and it never missed a beat and deserves far better than being stuck in a dark corner of our garage. I vow to have it returned to them by the time this book is published.

Big thanks to Berghaus who came up trumps with the backpacks. If it weren't for them we'd have had to carry our spare pants around in an old Tesco carrier bag. Ok, maybe that's stretching it a bit, but it would have been a lot harder work without two marvellous rucksacks to stash our beers in.

An ENORMOUS thank you is due to Rachel from Go Your Own Way Apparel who designed and printed our fabulous 'Tour T-shirts'. We absolutely loved them and they brought a smile to many a face when we were on our trek.

We are also incredibly grateful to everyone who supported us with accommodation and/or time and activities, your support means more to us than you'll probably ever know: Crumble Cottages, Distant Horizons (sadly no longer trading, but please don't blame us for that!), Grizedale Mountain Bikes, Suzannah Cruickshank, Sunnyside Guesthouse, Skiddaw Youth Hostel, St Bees School, Wordsworth House, Lake District Wildlife Park, The Lakeside and Haverthwaite Railway and Ravenglass and Eskdale Railway.

And finally to every single person who gave up their time to walk with us, thank you, thank you, THANK YOU! This would have been a really boring story without all of your fascinating input and support – we know how incredibly busy you all are and are just so very grateful you chose to spend time with us. We hope you enjoyed the lunatic adventure as much as we did.

How to make beer

Rather than bore you with eighteen brewery tours, one for each day of the hike, we thought it might be better to just tell you, up front, how to make beer. Well, the basic process at least; you see there may only be four main ingredients in beer – water, hops, yeast, grain (usually, but not always barley) – and one basic process, but it's the varieties of the ingredients, the differences in quantities and the various different sources, which make brewing an endlessly interesting dark art. And that's before we even mention the timings of each step, the water temperatures, how long brews are left at each step in the process etc. the variables are as infinite as they are mind boggling.

Most breweries (and certainly all the ones we visited) buy their grain already malted, this means it's been soaked in water, spread on a malting floor and allowed to germinate, dried in a kiln and then crushed to release the sugars.

Ingredients used in the beer-making process

The very basic steps:

1. Mashing – soak the malted grain in hot water to start the sugar fermenting to extract the fermentable sugars, colour and malt flavours. This is done in a Mash Tun.
2. Take the water (referred to as 'wort') from the mash, boil it and add the hops, adding hops at one, two or more stages.
3. Remove the hops, cool the water (wort) and move it to the fermenter.
4. Add the yeast and allow it to ferment – this can take several days and it's where the sugar turns into alcohol.
5. Skim the yeast off the top ready for the next brew.
6. When it's done fermenting, move the liquid beer to a conditioning tank and leave it for days, weeks or months, depending on what you're making.
7. Pop the liquid beer into a cask, or bottle.
8. Drink it!

Every brewery we spoke to recycle their by-products in some way, and there are few farm animals in Cumbria that aren't being fed on by-products of the brewing industry. It's the used grains that go to farms, known as 'brewers' grains' – the hops are more useful to gardeners for composting and mulch.

It is hard to believe that the endless array of beer varieties around the world all come from some variation in the process, and the four simple ingredients above. The type of hops, where it's grown, what the growing season has been like, when it was picked, how it's been kept, handled and stored, and how much is added, will all affect the flavour of the beer. It's the same for the other three ingredients; any tiny variation will affect the flavour and, for breweries that rely on consistency, that can be a real headache.

On top of all of that, each brewery will have a precise recipe for each brew; timings, temperatures, quantities etc., and many of these will be a closely guarded secret. Some of the most popular pints in the county are the result of years of meticulous research whereas others are the result of a very happy accident.

With such a vast quantity of variety on offer, it seemed a real

shame that we encountered so many stories of people demanding the same drink, again and again, and walking out of the pub if they didn't have it, rather than daring to try something new. Some folks have no sense of adventure.

How to use this book

This is not a walking book and we're certainly not expecting anyone to follow in our footsteps, but we've included the maps of our routes in case a stroll takes your fancy (beer cask optional) and, wherever they exist, the transportation links to get you back to your start point.

We've also told you where you can sup the brews we sampled although, as you'll see in the book, this can be a variable beast so, if in doubt, check their website first.

Some of the breweries offer tours and experiences and would welcome you with open arms should you decide to stop by, others brew up in their backyards and much as I am sure that they would love to share a pint with you, Health and Safety or other red tape, means they can't. Again, check their websites first, where you should find all the information you need.

You'll also notice that we a) haven't visited all the microbreweries in the county because, much as we would have loved to, there were simply far too many and b) had a couple of days which didn't feature a brewery, but the reasons for that will become perfectly clear when you read the book.

At the end of each chapter you'll find an overview of the brewery and their website address. We've also listed a few of their beers but please be aware that their offerings can change throughout the year, so please, again, visit their websites – or pop in and see them – to check out their full range. And also check out all the other amazing Cumbrian breweries – it really is an amazing county!

Finally, we've written this book in the form of dialogue between the two of us – you'll read me in black and Steve in blue italics!

At the top of Helvelyn

Prologue

HEAVEN KNOWS WE NEEDED A BEER or two in 2020/2021, and it was useful to know where all the best places to get one were.

Although assorted lockdowns and restrictions delayed the publication of this book, it's wonderful to see that pretty much all of the breweries kept right on going, with many showing tons of creativity, imagination and community spirit. Beer was being delivered to the doorstep in many locations and, as there has been a recent resurgence in doorstep milk deliveries, I reckon that getting your 'daily pinta beer' could definitely catch on!

I'll be honest, we really wanted to undertake some impressive stunt to include as an update in the book, but the reality is, as for many people, the COVID situation had a pretty devastating effect on our livelihoods, so we've been working like the clappers to keep on top of things.

Thankfully things are looking much brighter now although, sadly, we don't have a lot of time left over for doing strange and creative things with a beer cask, however much we would like to.

We've tweaked and updated the book where it was needed; they are mostly happy updates, but there was one notable exception which reminded us both that life is indeed short, so here's to having more crazy adventures and enjoying a beer or two with great friends. Cheers!

A long way up...

Ulverston

Ulverston Brewing
Company

Cartmel Sands

Beckside

Cartmel

Cark

Morecambe Bay

Another fine mess

 Start: The Bay Horse, Canal Foot, Ulverston

End: Cartmel

Distance: 8 miles/ 13KM

Terrain: Mostly tarmac

Transportation: Train – stations at Ulverston and Cark

I WOKE UP EXHAUSTED. It was 6am on day one of our hike and I was absolutely knackered. This was not how I imagined it. Unless you've ever undertaken a ridiculous long-distance hike you probably won't realise quite how much planning is required – I certainly didn't. Back in 2003 I'd arranged everything for our wedding within the space of eight weeks and barely missed a step, believe me when I tell you that was a walk in the park compared with the planning required to haul a beer cask around Cumbria.

Naively I'd thought that if I started organising everything in January then there'd be very little for me to worry about during the final few days, and certainly nothing I'd need to faff with while we were actually on the walk. Oh, how I laugh about that now, poor naive fool that I was.

On the Friday before our Sunday departure, I sat down at the laptop just before 8am thinking that I'd just sort a few last-minute emails etc. before lunch. By lunchtime I was swearing at the screen every few minutes and lunch was a bag of chicken crisps and two slices of ham straight from the packet. I eventually stepped away from the machine at 8pm and headed straight for the gin.

Still, it was all done now, wasn't it? Today was day one, the sun was shining, and we were about to set off, what could possibly need doing now? I switched on my phone, an email pinged in: 'Re the beer hike, I was wondering if there was any flexibility in the times or dates.'

'I TOLD YOU THE DAMNED DATES SIX MONTHS AGO' I yelled at the screen, before forcing myself to type something polite, with caps lock off … This was a scene that would be repeated on an almost daily basis …

After breakfast I packed and repacked my lovely Berghaus rucksack. Current weight: one tonne. I unpacked it again looking for things to exclude. I ditched the shampoo and a book I was reading and eyed my two epipens lying on the bed. I have an allergy to insect bites so need to keep them with me, but they're really quite heavy. I picked them up and pondered for a moment the choice between possible death and a lighter rucksack. It was a tougher call than it really should have been.

With our two rucksacks propped up in the hallway we had a childish 'mine's heavier than yours' competition, though why I was pleased to win that one is beyond me.

I think you'll find mine was heavier.

To be fair I think the only reason Steve's was a shade lighter was because his rucksack was a few years newer. When we told them about our adventure Berghaus had kindly sent us a new backpack for him, and it barely weighed a thing when it was empty.

We set off to the station, the short track outside our house giving us a taste of what it would be like hauling the cask uphill. Oh yes, didn't I mention? We'd not tried it out or anything. No dummy runs or checks that it was all ok. Nope. Day one we strapped it onto its trolley and off we set because that's just how we roll. Our track is twenty metres tops and it was hard work; I was already looking forward to Helvellyn.

Beth looking very fresh at the start of the adventure

Nah thought it would add to the adventure as we were reasonably assured we couldn't break it, 'Well you might need to take split pins if the wheels fall off but apart from that it's pretty indestructible!' At least that's what Nathan at Hesket Newmarket said when he loaned us the trolley.

Off we go...

Also the only recce I did beforehand was for the day where we would be meeting up with Debbie in her wheelchair, where there was potentially an issue with access. Now I've been up fells, I know what they look like, but when I got to the fell in question, that's when it hit me, whoa, that's going to be quite a trek dragging wheels up there ... At that point we still hadn't worked out how we were going to transport the cask, on a four-wheel trolley or a sack barrow maybe? We'd even looked at the strength of kiddy bike wheels attached to some sort of frame.

But, thanks to the nice folks at Hesket Newmarket, we now had the cask trolley and I'd bought some split pins, just in case. I knew holding a metal handle any distance wasn't going to be comfortable but luckily I had a length of pipe insulation. I wrapped it around the handles and it fitted perfectly. The cask was ready for his adventures!

Having man-handled it onto the train we did at least discover one upside of travelling with your own beer cask – it makes an excellent (if cumbersome) seat. Very handy when it comes to Northern Rail.

It didn't take long before we decided to give it a fitting name in more ways than one. Firkin Cask, on account of the fact that it held a Firkin of ale and it was, well, a cask. We may also have called it some similar sounding names during the hike ...

We describe ourselves as Nosey Hikers but today Beth was going to be a duck (well is she often quite quackers). No this time it was her rucksack, making a duck quacking sound each time she took a step. Would I be walking with a duck for the next 138 miles? Can I expect a row of

ducklings in tow? My brain wandered off into the weird, as it usually does, this time 'Follow the Beth' from the 1980s lager ad 'Follow the Bear'. And did you know Orson Welles directed those ads? And he was the voice behind Carlsberg's 'Probably the best lager ...'.

Anyways, it wasn't just Beth making a noise, the cask clanked over even the smallest of stones, this could be annoying, for us, anyone else within a one-mile radius and all the local wildlife. Not to worry, I have faith in our good friend Stewart, who we were staying with that evening. Meanwhile, 'Clank Clank Quack Quack Clank ...'

Our starting point was The Bay Horse at Canal Foot in Ulverston. Why there? Why not! Our gin hike had started from there and there was an excellent pub and brewery in the town, plus Lesley, the Landlady at The Bay Horse, had promised us lunch so it would have been churlish to refuse. Joining us at lunch were Anna (our lovely longsuffering publisher), her dog Maya and partner. Also joining us were Andy and Zoe from Shed 1 – we didn't know them at all before our gin hike and now we were firm friends; funny how ludicrous booze-fuelled adventures have a way of connecting people.

The Bay Horse is steeped in local history. Back in the day it was the start/ finishing point for folks crossing the bay. It would have been a focal point for the town, especially on market days, as people waited for the tides to drop before venturing out onto the sands. Lesley, and her partner Robert, have been there 30 years – Robert had previously been head chef at Miller Howe but they dreamed of owning their own pub and so, with support of Miller Howe owner John Tovey, they took on The Bay Horse.

The pub has a wonderful homely feel and is very much an integral part of the community. They open for coffee from 9am where locals will drop in to read the papers or have a natter. It's a favourite haunt for dog walkers and dogs have often been known to turn up without their owner and are welcomed with a treat and a bowl of water. There are some lovely old photos of past regulars on the walls and it's clear that the place is very dear to the hearts of all the regulars around Canal Foot and beyond.

When we visited Lesley was particularly excited as they'd just unveiled their brand-new pub sign – hand painted and resplendent in the sunshine. In an era of depressing pub chains The Bay Horse is a wonderfully refreshing place to visit, in every sense of the word (lunch was fabulous!).

I like Canal Foot and was glad we'd chosen to start there; it's a real hidden gem. As we stood on the shore I looked over to Chapel Island – it was hard to believe you could walk over there at low tide, when the tide is in it looks completely inaccessible. I think I'd quite like to live on an island. Maybe not on quite that remote though – would be a real pain getting beer over there, unless you built a pipeline, it wasn't that far from The Bay Horse, I wonder if it's doable?

Much as we could have sat there all afternoon, we had a brewery to visit and a train to catch. Not to mention six miles or so to hike. We headed out to take some fresh-faced start line photos – although, by now, I had gone beyond exhausted and was seriously considering giving everyone the slip and nipping off to the ladies for a crafty nap.

We had toyed with the idea of having a big send off on a pony and cart, but, with the myriad of other things going on we'd opted to spend time with the pony and cart one day earlier because we wanted to get the cask onto as many different forms of transport as possible. So far we'd not walked a single pace and had already logged train, trolley and horse drawn cart.

Lovely Tom

An easy gig...

The horse in the photo is Tom, a nine-year-old gypsy cob belonging to Vivien Greenhow and her partner Ian Flemming. They breed horses at their Newland Green stables and Tom was incredibly patient as we trotted to and fro in the sunshine taking photos and videos.

Vivien and Ian live on the outskirts of Ulverston and had kindly walked Tom around to the Bay Horse for us, I was a bit worried about how he'd cope in the heat, but they reassured me that he'd be fine. We did begin to draw a crowd though, something I'd have to get used to over the coming weeks, although I didn't know that then.

> Why couldn't we take the horse the whole way with us? It would have made things a lot easier. Many of the mountain passes and cross valley tracks are old communication routes so a horse drawn cart with a beer cask and two weary travellers on the back surely wouldn't have been an uncommon sight back in the day. We could have tented on the cart, or bivvied under the stars.

Photos done, nap still eluding me, we set off along the canal on the first steps of the walk. We were a merry band accompanied by Colin Smith from the Ulverston Canal Regeneration Group (UCRG) and what he doesn't know about the canal really isn't worth knowing. In a nutshell the canal is 1.25 miles long, 15 feet deep and 66 feet wide. Halfway along its diminutive length is a rolling bridge which is the only one of its kind in Europe.

The canal was completed in 1796 and, for a while, was an essential part of trade in Ulverston accommodating thousands of vessels during its lifetime. With its working life long behind it these days the canal provides a wonderful flat walk connecting Ulverston town to the coast and Colin and the UCRG work with the owners to ensure it remains safe, clean and a haven for wildlife. They have also provided the information boards and other informative objects and activities ensuring that this once vital part of the town's past is not forgotten.

After a few paces Colin asked, 'Beth are you trying to attract Ducks?' Ah good, not just me then ...

In October 2019 Colin invited us to join him at the unveiling of a 2m wide working, cast iron, model of the rolling bridge. An hour or so after the official festivities were done and dusted we walked back past the model and watched as a stream of folks stopped to investigate it and understand just how the bridge had worked; the UCRG have really helped to engage the community with the canal and helped everyone understand just what a wonderful asset it is.

We were also joined by Paul from Ulverston Brewing Company, our very first brewery! They first began producing beer in 2005 and have been on their present site since 2010 – their present site being the atmospheric old cattle market. Paul's brewing inspiration goes back to his school days when he'd watch the hops coming and going from

The old cattle market put to very good use

Hartley's Brewery opposite his school gates. Sadly, Hartley's Brewery closed in 1991 (the iconic buildings still remain and someone should really breathe life back into them!), a move which had been on the cards for a while but it set into motion an interesting chain of events ...

On 16 June 1990 Paul had attended a 'Sons of the Desert' party to celebrate what would have been Stan Laurels 100th birthday (Stan was born in Ulverston and the Sons of the Desert are the official Laurel and Hardy Society). At midnight they all sang 'Lonesome Pine' together before Paul wandered off home alone, his head swimming with ideas. As he walked he realised that 'Lonesome Pine', 'Laughing Gravy' and other Laurel and Hardy themed names would make excellent names for beers. He'd always wanted to make beer but hadn't found anyone to join him, yet ...

I remember watching Harold Lloyd films after school along with all the Laurel and Hardy films, I always loved the stunts they performed. Had no idea at the time that Stan Laurel was born so near to where I was living (I was in Kents Bank back then). Did you know Bill Hailey's mum was also born in Ulverston?

Fast forward to 2000 and he met Anita. They began making beer in their garage, the proper stuff, not from kits. As they gained skills and confidence they decided to 'go for it'. Anita had been visiting the Prince of Wales pub in Foxfield (see chapter 18) to learn how to make beer

The magic starts here

commercially and in 2005 Paul left behind his nice steady job at Glaxo SmithKline and launched into the world of beer production. Today they brew just shy of 100 casks per week and sell most of their beers within a twenty-mile radius. Most notably they supply a range of beers to the Haverthwaite steam railway, which are perennially popular with visitors. True to Paul's original idea most of their beers are named in honour of Laurel and Hardy.

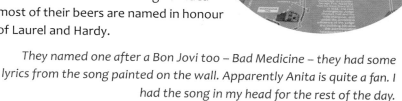

They named one after a Bon Jovi too – Bad Medicine – they had some lyrics from the song painted on the wall. Apparently Anita is quite a fan. I had the song in my head for the rest of the day.

We forced ourselves (obviously being too polite to refuse) to drink a pint of Laughing Gravy, a dark amber, pleasingly malty beer, before weaving out into the sunshine and back to the station. Our final mission of the day was to hop on a train to Cark then walk up to Cartmel and our bed for the night.

Cask #056

I decided I should rename Cask #056 each day so, to honour Laurel and Hardy I decided to name him, 'Another Fine Cask'. Though perhaps the cask was thinking more on the line of 'On the wrong trek'.

There's a nasty sharp hill up out of Cark which we cursed our way up before following the Cistercian Way into the village. Our bed was at Crumble Cottages, a pair of stunning holiday cottages, lovingly restored by our good friends Stewart and Sarah – folks we'd only got to know thanks to our gin hike.

Never mind the 'nasty hill', have you forgotten about the stairs at Ulverston Station? Plenty of clattering and banging (and quacking), as we tried to get to the platform, and lots of odd looks too.

Over the past five years or so Stewart and Sarah, doing much of the work themselves, have bashed, beaten and coaxed these previously run down cottages, turning them into two properly perfect romantic holiday lets. The cottages are surrounded by stunning gardens, which they have also restored and lucky guests arrive to freshly cut garden flowers and, if they want it, a basket of home grown fruit and veg. Real Cumbrian getaways don't get more idyllic than that.

With each step our rucksacks felt heavier as we plodded out of the village towards our final destination. As we rounded a bend we bumped into someone Steve knew from his conservation work parties with Cumbria Wildlife Trust.

'Hello weary hikers!' came the greeting.

This was day one. Admittedly the end of day one but we still had seventeen more days and a LOT of hills to go; if I looked as knackered as I felt then maybe this wasn't such a great plan. We paused for a chat before continuing on and collapsing in a heap on Stewart and Sarah's doorstep. The very best thing about friends is they always know exactly what's needed and Sarah took me by the hand and showed me the prettiest table of gins and garnishes I ever did see, then ordered me to drink, put my feet up and jettison half my rucksack.

Following a sumptuous dinner, me and Sarah went through my rucksack together and she ruthlessly made me turf out a good third of the contents. She was bang on about most of them, but I still may not forgive her for making me ditch my hair conditioner.

One of the many draft beers available from Ulverston Brewing Company

While Beth and Sarah sorted out the rucksacks, I sought some DIY assistance from Stewart in his Wonderous Imaginarium, his Emporium of tools and gadgets. Otherwise known as his shed. (More of a barn really, to be fair.) I'm sure he's 'Doc' Brown on the side, inventing time travelling gadgets on the quiet. 'Great Scott!' Well he is Scottish, as it goes.

I needed it silent and I needed it quick release, that was the brief. With that, he ditched my pathetic straps and replaced them with an industrial strength ratchet strap that could take on any challenge. Some thick foam padding was also installed for a comfortable, and silent, ride. Bliss. Apart from Beth's quacking ...

Later on, sinking into the fresh clean sheets on the enormously comfy bed, I pondered the challenges that lay ahead for a full ten seconds or so before falling fast asleep.

BREWERY: Ulverston Brewing Company

WEBSITE: ulverstonbrewingcompany.co.uk

BEERS: Laughing Gravy, Lonesome Pine, Pink Elephant, Bad Medicine

TOURS? By prior appointment only

TAP ROOM? Yes, by appointment only

STOCKED: Local shops & bars and Lakeside & Haverthwaite Railway

Lakeside
Windermere
Lakeside and Haverthwaite Railway
Haverthwaite
Bigland Tarn
Beckside
Cartmel
Unsworth's Brewery

Full steam ahead

- **Start**: Crumble Cottages, Cartmel
- **End**: Lakeside Jetty
- **Distance**: 5 miles/ 8KM
- **Terrain**: Tarmac, hard track, soft ground
- **Transportation**: Train – Bus routes X6 and 532

DESPITE ALL THE ACTIVITIES of day one, I woke up on day two feeling far less exhausted. Crumble Cottages are a divine peaceful retreat lovingly restored by Stewart and Sarah; it feels like you're in the middle of nowhere but you're just a mile from the heart of Cartmel and its fine array of world-renowned food and drink establishments. One of their cottages even has a hot tub where you can relax in the hot bubbles under the stars with a glass of cold fizz, and if that's not romantic heaven then I don't know what is.

Sarah whipped us up a fortifying bacon sarnie to set us up for the hike ahead and promised to pack us some lunch while we were out visiting Unsworth's Brewery down in the village. We set off feeling light as a feather with the cask but no rucksacks; I was already beginning to understand why people on long distance hikes pay good money to have someone transport their main pack from one stop to the next, something I'd always previously dismissed as cheating.

Casky was running silent. Stewart's amazing interventions had worked a treat and we were now in full stealth mode.

Unsworth's had been kind enough to loan us the cask for this crazy mission so it was only right that we paid them a visit nice and early on. If I were to ask you to describe the perfect setting for a brewery, there's a very good chance you'd come up with something pretty close to what Unsworth's have achieved. They share a small courtyard with several

At Unsworth's Yard

other businesses, most notably a cheese emporium and an artisan bread shop which also produces divine wood fired pizzas. As if all that wasn't enough there's also Windermere Wines, owned and run by another member of the Unsworth's clan, where you can buy a fabulous bottle of wine to enjoy with your beer, pizza, bread and cheese. See – I told you it was the perfect setting, didn't I?

Throughout the summer every Friday and Saturday night is Beer & Pizza night in the courtyard, often with live music. There's a giant umbrella to cover the entire yard in the event of rain and a nice big fire pit to keep everyone warm and toasty. They've even launched an annual music event which they've called 'Unstock' – three days of pizza and music (as opposed to Woodstock's three days of peace and music). The whole place is a glorious hub of food, drink and loveliness.

The Unsworth family once ran the Cartmel village garage and now own the brewery where they have an agreement with the Harrington family to use the name and heritage behind the 'Last Wolf' beer. The local legend suggests that the last wolf in England was killed at Humphrey Head in the fourteenth century by John, son of Sir Edgar Harrington of Wraysholme Tower, after he chased it from Cartmel Forest (now known as Grizedale forest). You can also see the wolf in their family crest and as a gold wolf's head weathervane on Cartmel Priory.

When we visited they had not long launched their new beer 'Eel River IPA', named after the local river Eea which is Viking for Eel (and there are still eels in it – the river, not the beer!). Prior to setting off on the hike me and Steve would have described ourselves as not particularly knowledgeable beer drinkers – we both enjoyed beer but didn't really understand the difference between 'ale', 'beer', 'lager', 'IPA' etc., we knew they all tasted different, but we didn't know why. We were about to get our first lessons.

An IPA is an India Pale Ale and they are generally stronger (alcohol-wise) and have a more bitter taste than other beers. It was invented by the British in the days of the Empire when our attempts at sending beer by boat to India failed because the beer went off before it got there. Alcohol and hops both act as preservatives so it was discovered that if beer had a higher alcohol content and more hops, it would last long enough to make it all the way to India.

These days, of course, we have refrigeration so the original reasons for creating the IPA are long gone, but it remains a popular drink. Our mission was to sample as many local beers as we could so, despite it being only 10am, we toasted the ingenuity of our magnificent country which dedicated a good chunk of time and energy into ensuring that our ex-pats on a far flung continent could still enjoy a beer from home. I have to say that half a pint of IPA is just the thing to set you up for a full day of hiking and would make a welcome addition to any breakfast buffet.

It's beer o'clock somewhere

Archimedes' Principle and the leaky bung:

One of my many concerns with the cask was during the swimming day and whether the cask would guarantee to float. My swimming proficiency lessons only went as far as retrieving a brick. Though should the cask sink like one, I'm not sure I would be able to salvage it from the murky depths of Rydal Water. I had hammered in the official cask bung as provided by Peter so wanted to double check with him that it was securely in. He assured us it would float. 'That bung is going nowhere, well it's all about the Archimedes' Principle. If he's wrong all metal ships would sink'.

Basically, the buoyant upward force applied by the water on an object is equal to the weight of the water displaced by the object. So the weight of a hollow air tight cask is the same as the displaced weight of water, so it ~~should~~ will float. Ok the physics seems sound, you know you feel you should have complete trust in the old science bloke but you can't help having doubts. Titanic drifted across my mind ...

Again Peter assured us the cask was pretty indestructible, making various suggestions. Challenge accepted. Peter really shouldn't be giving us ideas. Hmm I have an idea. Dam Busters ...

Back at Crumble Cottages we surveyed the huge pile of sarnies that Sarah had prepared for lunch. And the cake. And the freshly made flasks of tea. I did try to persuade her to follow us along the entire hike, or at least pop in and see us every morning with our supplies, but she muttered something about having two holiday cottages and a garden design business to run. Spoilsport.

We all set out towards Newby Bridge and Stewart won my undying devotion when he strapped my rucksack to the top of the cask and insisted on pulling the whole thing himself. The first stretch wasn't too bad as we followed the road until it ran out. Then we literally hit our first hurdle – our first stile to navigate. Steve, Stewart and Sarah figured out the best way to tackle it, while I helpfully hung back and took photos while shouting words of encouragement and giggling.

'Ow!' I shouted.

'What?' Steve paused mid-stile, cask and trolley aloft.

'I've been clegged!' I shouted back, adding a few swear words for good measure and peering at the rapidly expanding red lump on my arm. 'Clegg' is the local name for the horsefly and, if you've ever been bitten by one, you'll understand the swearing. I'm also allergic to insect bites and have been blue lighted for gnat bites in the past (hence the epipens), so you can imagine my annoyance. The only antihistamine which works for me is Piriton, which also knocks me out, but I had no choice other than to launch a pre-emptive Piriton strike and hope for the best.

I was pleased with how the cask and trolley were performing. Our first outing over properly 'lumpy' terrain and the new straps held firm. It was also our first attempt at getting the cask up and over stiles and kissing gates too. The whole hike really made us stop and think about accessibility – easy enough for us to hoik a cask and trolley up and over an obstacle, but not so easy with a wheelchair.

Very cheerful at the first stile

Deer at 11 o'clock!

As we continued up the track we spotted a group of deer and magnificent stag sitting on a nearby crag. However often you see something like that, it never gets old and we all stood still and watched until they got wind of us and moved on.

A little later on we paused for lunch and although we all wolfed down a good pile of sarnies and cake; we barely dented the mountain Sarah had prepared for us. She insisted we take all the leftover bits with us, for which I was incredibly grateful as we could have them for tea later on. These sorts of adventures are fantastic fun but don't come cheap so anything that saved us cash was most welcome.

Our destination was Haverthwaite Station and a ride on the Lakeside and Haverthwaite Steam Railway. We were all childishly excited! Although now only a seventeen-minute ride the line was once part of the great railway network in the region, originally to ship coal to the Windermere steamers before evolving into a popular visitor attraction. The station at Haverthwaite has a fabulous tearoom serving lovely homemade food (including divine cream teas!) and we

Looking over the River Leven

STEAM IN LAKELAND

FAIRBURN ALE

alc 4.0% vol

Alversteiner
Pilsner

*A dream
cream tea*

A most picturesque place

also noted the range of beers made by Ulverston Brewing Company which we'd discovered yesterday.

They had their Fairburn Ale too – and don't forget to try the Fairburn Ale Cumberland sausages either.

This line was also home to 'Old Coppernob', an 0-4-0 (for steam train aficionados), built in 1846, and named because of its large copper firebox. In 1941 its copper 'nob' was damaged by an air-raid when bombers targeted Barrow-in-Furness, and the damage is still visible today. These days it's in the safe care of the Science Museum.

I think everyone gets excited by a steam train. It might be steaming it down with rain but it doesn't stop the visitors! Not that it was steaming down when we visited, quite the opposite in fact. A bit of rain would have been nice and cool.

As we stood with the crowds on the platform craning our necks to see the train arrive, I wondered why we never got this excited about rail travel any more. (Although, to be fair, I do get wildly excited anytime my Northern Rail train arrives on time, but that's not very often.) We take travel for granted these days, even flying is a dull necessity for many – we all want to be in places but we've lost the pleasure of getting there.

We all piled into the final carriage of the train, technically it may have been the old Guard's Van, but it had bench seats around the edges and huge windows around three sides making it feel like we were in a conservatory on wheels. I scampered around all the windows admiring the views – I'd had no idea how wide the river was at that point – and I was quite sad when we chuffed into Lakeside station. We bid Stewart and Sarah farewell and made our way to the B&B where we just had time to freshen up before being whisked away to Lake District Radio for an interview.

Generating publicity for a project like this is essential – particularly as we were raising funds for Mountain Rescue – and we were lucky that much of the local press had picked up on our adventure. We'd also spent time chatting to BBC Radio Cumbria up in Carlisle before we set off, and now we were to be interviewed by Cumbria's newest radio station.

I was looking forward to this part. Obviously I knew that Beth was doing a radio show, and here was my chance to see just what it was she got up to and what the studio looked like. It was smaller than I imagined. We've done quite a few interviews with BBC Lancashire and BBC Cumbria in their fancy big studios, but this is much smaller. After we lost Lakeland Radio and The Bay, it was nice to see someone try to plug the gap. I'm always quite nervous about these things, but Beth seemed right at home and I was glad she did most of the talking.

The Lakeside and Haverthwaite Steam Railway: only the finest of transportation for our Casky

Our destination, Lakeside

At the time of our visit Lake District Radio was just ten weeks old and today I am one of their regular presenters. The station broadcasts from the YMCA centre on Windermere and Plumgarths studios in Kendal and all of the presenters are local and nuts about good music. It came into being to fill the void left when two previous local stations were sold off to Heart and Smooth and immediately ceased being local – the really sad part was they closed the local studios and, as well as a lot of people losing their jobs, we also lost a bit of our local history and identity. Lake District Radio plays a range of music as well as having plenty of competitions, live music events and outside broadcasts.

We were interviewed by Steve Guppy, the then station manager, who was keen to know what prompted us to undertake such a ridiculous adventure. In some ways we had a lot of reasons but in other ways just the one – it seemed like fun, so why not?

Interview over Steve dropped us back at our B&B where we polished off the remainder of sarnies and cake prepared for us by Sarah. For dessert I enjoyed Piriton and tea with a light Anthisan sauce on my rapidly expanding clegg bite. Tomorrow we were to canoe half the length of Windermere, what could possibly go wrong?

I'll be honest, I was beginning to worry about the canoeing. We've only ever had a couple of outings and Windermere is a big lake – the biggest in

England, in fact. I was glad we'd got a good guide with us, but I couldn't help wondering if we could make a late change to one of those nice big boats with a bar onboard …

BREWERY: Unsworth's Yard Brewery

WEBSITE: unsworthsyard.co.uk/brewery

BEERS: Last Wolf, Eel River IPA, Sandpiper

TOURS? Pop in anytime, not so much a tour as a 'pop your head though the door and see the tanks'.

TAP ROOM? Yes, open throughout the year

STOCKED: Local shops & bars and served in L'Enclume

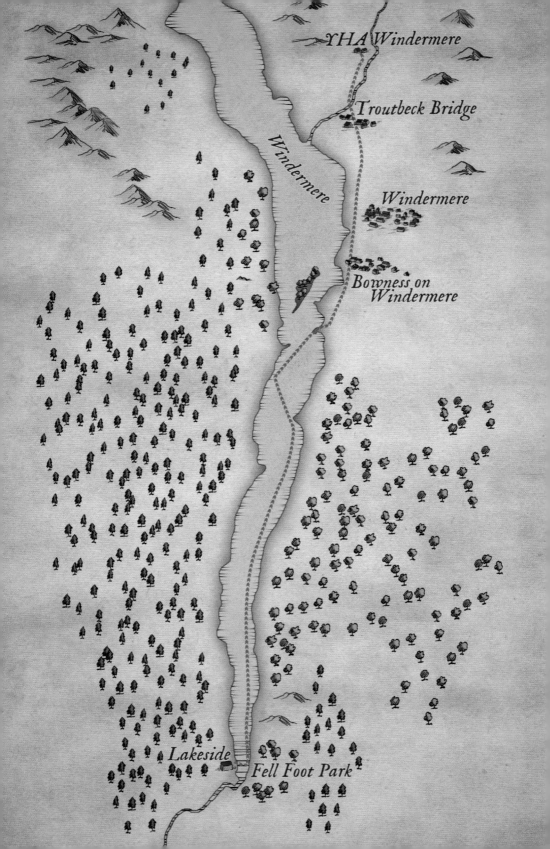

YHA Windermere

Troutbeck Bridge

Windermere

Windermere

Bowness on
Windermere

Lakeside

Fell Foot Park

Row, row, row your boat

- **Start:** Fell Foot Park, Windermere
- **End:** Bowness-on-Windermere
- **Distance:** 6.5 miles/ 10.5KM by canoe
- **Terrain:** Mostly water
- **Transportation:** Windermere Lake Cruises – regular service throughout the year

THE CLEGG BITE HAD MORPHED from the size of a large pea (possibly mushy) into a golf ball, minus the dimples. I'd had another good night's sleep and needed to be wide awake for the long paddle ahead of us, but a dose of Piriton* was non-negotiable. I quickly swallowed one down then headed off to enjoy a magnificent full breakfast; with six miles of canoeing ahead I needed all the calories I could muster. Our lovely landlord at Landing Cottage B&B made a generous donation to our Mountain Rescue tin and waved us on our way.

First up was the easy part, meeting our old friend James from Windermere Lake Cruises who had arranged for us to cadge a lift over to Fell Foot Park where our canoes awaited! The larger boats steam up and down the entire length of the lake offering a wonderfully relaxed way to take in the scenery with your feet up and a coffee and cake firmly in hand, but we were doing things the hard way. We were taking the small ferry across from Lakeside to Fell Foot – just five minutes by boat but a twenty to thirty-minute drive or several hours of hiking – and then getting into an even smaller boat to canoe six miles up the lake to Bowness.

---

* Editor's note: it is inadvisable to mix antihistamines with alcohol.

Each time we meet James we have to apologise to him. In 2014 we played an April Fool's Joke with Windermere Cruises where we wrote a blog claiming that they offered submarine tours through the newly discovered underwater limestone caverns under Windermere. They still get asked about those. Sorry James. Sorry Windermere Cruises.

We couldn't help noticing a brisk wind whipping down the lake and hoped it wouldn't affect our canoe trip too much. The ferry pulled in and, while James and Steve figured out the best way to get the cask aboard I chatted to the ferryman.

'Nasty north wind today,' he said. 'Where are you off to?'

'We're canoeing up to Bowness.'

'Into this wind? Rather you than me.'

The cask was safely deposited on deck as the ferryman's assistant arrived.

'These two are canoeing all the way up to Bowness today,' the ferryman informed him.

'Into this wind?' the assistant looked at me.

'Yes, it'll be fine, we've got an escort,' I smiled, although my confidence was bobbing up and down like the boats on the lake. One second I was brimming over with the excitement of the adventure and a 'let's take on the world' bravado, the next I was wondering what the hell we were getting ourselves into and why weren't we taking one of those nice big boats with all the seats and onboard bar?

Who needs an onboard bar when you have the lake lapping at your feet and a bottle of Bowness Bay to warm your cockles?

Ready to row!

Stewart had made putting on the industrial straps look easy, and it probably was, but we were trying to take them off in a hurry and I couldn't figure out how. You know how it is, if you have loads of time then you can probably figure it out, but when you're racing to get it done before your boat pulls out, it's a whole different matter. In the end we dumped the cask and trolley onto the deck still attached to each other and opted to figure it out on the way over. Obviously, once there was no sense of urgency, the straps came off first time.

We arrived at Fell Foot and wandered off to find our guide for the day, Emma, and our two trusty canoes. As Emma busied herself getting everything ready, I hung around feeling useless and watched the wind pushing the waves against the shore.

'Are you keen kayakers then?' James enquired.

'Erm … nope … we've been out twice with Emma's gang in the past, but that's it.'

James may well have tried to hide his look of surprise but, if he did, he failed. Sarah and Stewart were with us again, this time helping with the logistics of getting the right people and kit into the right place for the day's activities. Sarah handed me another huge bag full of sandwiches

With Emma and our precious load
(not just the sandwiches)

and cakes – she really is a truly wonderful woman. I was determined to make myself useful so decided to help pack our stuff onto the canoe. I clutched my precious bag full of food and approached the canoe to stash it somewhere safe – I studied the canoe for a moment.

'Emma, 'I eventually ventured. 'Which end is the front?'

I swear I heard James stifle a giggle.

Sarah looked concerned, 'Will you two be Ok?' she asked.

My bravado returned. 'Yes, absolutely fine!' I replied, safely positioning our lunch into the spot indicted by Emma.

Lifejackets belted on, all goods and cask aboard, we set off on our voyage. I was in the front seat, responsible for lots of paddling and Steve was behind me, responsible for lots of paddling plus steering. Emma was alongside in her canoe, reassuringly attached to us forming a catamaran, with the cask and was responsible for making sure we all got to Bowness in one piece.

And they're off...

Boaty McCask Face

Ready for his maiden voyage and weighing roughly the same as an eight-year-old. There was no need to worry about how low the draft of the canoe would be (ooh get me and my canoeing terms); also not to be confused with draft beer that's served from casks/kegs and not bottles, even though you can get draft bottled beers but they just taste and look like cask beers but aren't actually. Confused with my brain's train of thought? I know I am.

Emma is a fabulous guide, full of energy, expertise and, most importantly, confidence. She runs outdoor adventure company Distant Horizons, based on Ullswater. We've been out with them a few times in the past and tried out both canoeing and kayaking along Ullswater. We even ventured out with our teenage nephews on one occasion and managed to wear them out in the space of a few hours, and if that's not worth a few quid, then I don't know what is!

It was an adventurous paddle, especially for novices such as ourselves, and particularly pushing directly into a headwind, but Emma kept a watchful eye on us and expertly navigated us along the shoreline, spotting plenty of sheltered bays where we could pull in for a rest when we were flagging.

Also it depends on how much it has rained and how high the lake is. The south end of Windermere runs out as the River Leven and into

Morecambe Bay. To alleviate flooding, the weir at Newby Bridge is opened which can make canoeing a little more adventurous. Good job we weren't heading that way. At least we weren't planning to. If that wind got much stronger it was a distinct possibility.

It turns out that Emma wasn't all that outdoorsy as kid, she mucked around on her bike but that was about it. It wasn't until she worked at PGL holidays one summer that she really got into the outdoors.

Back home in Cumbria she started off as an admin assistant at Distant Horizons before moving up the ranks and taking over running the organisation when the original owner moved on. These days she looks after a whole team of freelancers who guide everyone from rank beginners to adventurous experts as they seek out new and exciting ways to explore the Lake District. They also guide corporate groups and push them outside their comfort zones and enable them to have fun finding new ways to work together and build team strengths.

Despite Emma's continual positive encouragement my motivation did flag a couple of times, most notably a couple of hours into our journey when I was so sure that we were within striking distance of Bowness, but then we passed a hotel which I knew was only about halfway there. By a random fluke of chance we paddled past Toby, a good friend of ours, who had his hands full guiding a group of teenagers, also out in canoes, but without beer casks.

Steve was doing a fabulous job guiding the canoe and shouting occasional words of encouragement as we careered north, and not swearing too much each time my paddle slipped and I splashed him. All accidental, honest. Well, mostly …

Yeah, right.

There's a little more concentration required tandeming a canoe catamaran, matching oar strokes, speed, side and strength. The bows scanned the horizon left to right and back, just pick a side, either oar. It was hard work but great fun. Not sure Boaty had found his sea legs but certainly didn't pitch in, just enjoyed the ride. Canoe believe it?

Eventually we pulled in behind a large stone jetty.

'We'll have a proper rest here,' Emma instructed, 'and then we'll push for the finish – it's an open stretch with no hiding places so best have something to eat.'

Having swiftly wolfed down a couple of Sarah's sarnies and half a flask of tea, we declared ourselves ready. I knew how Scott must have felt when he made his final push for the South Pole. Except that our lives weren't in danger, we'd had plenty to eat, there was no blizzard blowing and we hadn't just eaten our ponies. Apart from that, I knew exactly how he must have felt.

We bounced, bobbed and swore our way into Bowness and attracted more than a few odd glances as we navigated around all the fancy boats in the marina in our two canoes with a beer cask in tow. Much as I wanted nothing more than to collapse in a heap and enjoy a nice long rest, we had an appointment to keep with Bowness Bay Brewing, so we bid the lovely Emma farewell and hauled our cask on into the town.

Manoevering around the marina was a bit scary, all those boats don't look very big from the shore, but when you're in a tiny canoe picking your way around them, they suddenly seem a lot bigger. It took us a couple of goes to find the right spot and there was James waiting for us. This time we had to apologise for being late, it may have taken a little longer than expected – he was waiting patiently with our rucksacks. Sorry James.

Thanks James (sorry James)

Richard Husbands was waiting for us in the Angel Inn and greeted us with the three little words every girl longs to hear; 'Fancy a pint?' I was smitten. With the cask safely stashed and a pint in our hands we got to chatting about the brewery.

Bowness Bay started up in 2012. After brewing at home for a while, Richard found that his beer was genuinely sought after by mates and a couple of local pubs. Richard had been making home brew in his garage for years and sharing it with his family and friends when he was made aware of some 'proper brewing kit' which became available in Norwich, so he bought it and Bowness Bay was born. And it's a proper family affair too; his wife Kim is the designer who designed all their pump clips and all of the Point of Sale information.

Richard has lived in Bowness for over twenty years and that's reflected in the names of the beers – they are mostly named after the Windermere boats that cruise up and down the lake: Swan Blonde, Tern IPA etc., and it's a brewery with big plans. Building on their solid reputation for excellent ales they have invested in state of the art kit and are expanding rapidly in Cumbria and the North West with plans to expand throughout the UK market and also venturing into exporting their beers. In July 2019 they opened their 'tap house' in Kendal ('The Barrel House' where you can take a tour of the brewery and enjoy all of their beers with a great plate of food from Joey's Cafe, next door).

I had a pint of Swan Blonde. Very nice. I like a nice light ale and this hit the spot perfectly. I also liked that fact that people kept giving us free beer. Maybe I should drag a cask around with me more often.

Also look out for their beer wagon which will mosey on in at outdoor events.

Much as they are pursuing global dreams they are still firmly rooted in Bowness and are staunch supporters of local events and activities and are always keen to give something back to the community. In that vein Richard gave us a little something to keep us going in the shape of six bottles of beer, a wonderful, if weighty, gift. Our only option was to empty them swiftly, purely for practical purposes you understand.

Wandering back down to the marina, all we had to do now was find our bed for the night, Windermere Youth Hostel. It couldn't be far out of Windermere, could it? Turns out, yes it could.

The Youth Hostel is thatta way...

'How far?' Steve craned his neck to try and see my phone screen.

'Three miles.'

'Three miles? Are you sure?'

I turned the screen so he could get a better look.

'Didn't you check when you booked it?' he asked, staring at the phone.

'Well, yes, I knew it was a bit out of town, I just didn't twig quite how far it was.' I looked at the screen willing the '3' in '3 miles' to change to a 2, or a 1 or even a 0, but it didn't. We both sighed heavily.

'Buses?' he asked

'Nothing for another hour.'

We looked at the screen again.

'They really shouldn't call it "Windermere Youth Hostel" should they?' I said 'Not when it's clearly in Troutbeck.'

There was nothing else for it; we had to walk.

Beth nipped into the nearby supermarket to buy some extra snacks. As I waited outside, a couple who had seen us earlier and wanted to come back to speak to us, how nice was that! The guy was into his beer and I couldn't believe when he asked for a selfie, with little ol' me, before kindly making a donation to our Mountain Rescue cause.

We wearily set off along the road towards Troutbeck. Along the way we paused on a bench in a car park overlooking the top of Windermere to finish off the final sarnies from Sarah and direct someone to 'Windermere

Sleep is thatta way...

Lake' – despite it being the largest lake in England, and them being on the road alongside it, they couldn't seem to find it. Given my cock-up with our accommodation for the evening, I was hardly in any position to judge.

Having trekked three miles to the hostel, I can't tell you how delighted we both were to discover that our room was on the first floor, just at the top of a particularly steep flight of steps. I did notice a stair lift and attempted to get it working, but we needed a key from reception and I didn't have the nerve to go and ask for it, so we dug deep and hauled it up to our final resting place for the day and crashed out in a stinky heap on the beds.

Thanks to the clegg bite my elbow was now the size of a tennis ball (I was going to say 'small tennis ball' but they're all the same size, aren't they?), so I smeared on the Anthisan and washed down my Piriton pill with a bottle of Swan Blonde and drifted off into an unwashed, smelly, sleep.

We really were exhausted. After a while we came down to the communal kitchen for a snack and a brew and I remember sitting outside on the benches looking down over a distant Windermere (the lake, not the town) with the evening sun on our faces. There was no wind up on the fells either by the looks of it as clouds hung close and motionless below the summits.

A beautiful view from the hostel of the distance we'd come

I also remember the bunk beds, and the interesting historical photos on the walls, and the fact that it was nowhere near Windermere.

On our way up we'd passed a very flash hotel with its own helipad. I know Beth was keen to take the cask on as many different types of transport as possible, all I had to do now was find someone with a helicopter, ideally someone who could drop us off in Windermere in the morning.

BREWERY: Bowness Bay Brewing

WEBSITE: bownessbaybrewing.co.uk

BEERS: Swan Blonde, Tern IPA, Swallow Gold, Swan Black, Lakes Lager, Amazon Amber, Lakeland Blonde, Raven Red, Swan Gold

TOURS? By prior appointment only

TAP ROOM? Yes, The Barrel House in Kendal

STOCKED: Local shops & bars and served in various pubs in Bowness, including The Angel Inn

Tour de Windermere

- **Start:** Bowness-on-Windermere
- **End:** Ambleside
- **Distance:** 7 miles/ 11KM by bike
- **Terrain:** Hard track
- **Transportation:** Windermere Lake Cruises – regular service throughout the year

I LAY IN BED and pulled back the curtains. The view from the room was spectacular, there was no denying it; I am sure that there are hotels in the Lake District charging a lot more money than we paid for views that don't even come close. We pootled downstairs for breakfast; the sun was shining, the patio was calling, so out we went to enjoy an alfresco breakfast in the sunshine, with more glorious views along the top end of Windermere. Honestly, I am unable to fault anything about this youth hostel other than its name. It is not. In. Windermere. But it is very lovely.

Sleep-walking to our destiny

I'd also woken up with a dehydration headache – due to under consumption of water rather than over consumption of beer. In an effort to make amends I guzzled plenty of tea and fruit juice and then immediately began worrying about how and where I'd pee all day. We had an early start as we had three miles to walk down into Bowness to catch the ferry (and had I mentioned that the youth hostel was a little out of town?) and pick up our bikes for the day.

As a mountain biker I was really looking forward to today. Beth would be the first to say that she's not hugely confident on a bike, mainly due to her appalling sense of balance – seriously she can, and does, trip over anything, but today was going to be a nice straightforward ride along the shores of Windermere. I was also keen to see what it would be like cycling with a kiddie carrier on the back.

Aboard the cask-craft

We timed our arrival at the ferry perfectly, explaining to a few people along the way just what it was that we were doing. It's hard to sneak around when you're carrying huge rucksacks and being closely followed by a cask of beer. As we boarded the ferry the guy taking the money asked what we were up to and, when we explained, he refused to take our fare and told us to put the money into our collecting pots instead, which we immediately did.

We were met on the other side by our chariots for the day, provided by Grizedale Mountain Bikes who had very kindly agreed to meet us off the ferry, loan us the bikes, carry our trolley and rucksacks and then

Fun for all the family

meet us again up in Ambleside when we were done. Perfect! 'But how will you carry a beer cask on a bike?' I hear you cry! Well, that would be what the child carrier is for – our beer cask weighed roughly the same as a small child but had the added benefit of not complaining when we hit a bump a bit hard.

Prior to setting off on our adventure we'd chatted to Pat McGucken, the manager, to find out a bit more about what they did, and I was really surprised at his response. I'd expected him to talk about helping crazy outdoors types have gnarly adventures in the hills, but instead his focus was on inclusivity and how they could ensure whole families could enjoy cycling through the woods together.

'One day a large family group came in, about fourteen of them,' he explained. 'One lady, probably the grandmother, was 70 and said she would love to join them but had had two hip replacements so was planning to kill three hours in the cafe while the others went out on their bikes. I could see she really wanted to join in so suggested she have a go on an electric bike.

'She wasn't too sure at first, but had ridden a bike in her youth so decided to give it a go. We took her out to the first cattle grid and back, only a few hundred yards, but she loved it. In the end she went out with the others and spent three hours cycling with the family. The look on her face when she came back was priceless. She was so happy that she'd not missed out on all the fun!'

Pat and his team make huge efforts to make cycling as accessible as they possibly can and are currently exploring trikes and other trailers for their bikes so more families can go adventuring together.

Back on the shores of Windermere we got the bikes set up and, after a few practice laps of the carpark, we were off! Windermere may be the longest lake in England but there aren't many stretches of the shoreline that are accessible to the public; but the route from Far Sawry up to Wray Castle is perfect for a gentle stroll or a rather lovely bike ride.

The kiddie carrier wasn't as tricky as I expected. Yes, it made the bike a bit heavier and slower (that was my excuse anyway), but after a while I barely noticed it was there. It was mainly when we stopped and started that it could be a bit awkward, and we stopped and started a lot, thanks to folks wanting to stop and chat and pop money in our collecting tins.

We set off at a gentle pace – we hadn't been able to strap the cask down and Steve was worried that it might roll away, but it proved to be surprisingly stable. It was a very stop/ start journey with folks stopping us every few hundred yards, asking what we were up to and putting money in our collecting tins.

'Oh, we saw someone hauling a cask like that along the road to Troutbeck yesterday,' said one couple.

'Yes, that was us …'

On our way to Wray

A scenic stop

Danny MacCaskill

If you are into mountain biking then you probably know who Danny MacAskill is and, if you don't, go and Google him now. I'll wait. He is an amazing trails biker and has done some cool and funny films like 'The Ridge' and 'Wee Day Out'. I thought it would be fun to get some photos of me re-enacting a funny moment from one of his films when he jumps his bike onto a haybale as it rolls down the hill, but instead we'd use a rolling cask. Ok I bottled out of any real action shots. We had attracted enough attention already without ending on a 'stunt shot gone wrong mishap video'. Looking at the kiddie carrier, I thought he should do another funny video with a carrier attached. When we returned home, it turned out that he had just made one, 'Danny Daycare' – definitely worth a watch.

Eat your heart out, Danny

Are we nearly there yet?!

The weather was amazing and the views were superb and cycling through the woods meant that we never got too hot. I know Steve had a few fun encounters with other families with kiddie trailers who were somewhat surprised when they saw the contents of ours. One even offered to swap ...

Aye, that was a funny moment. We were cycling one way and a family was cycling the other. The guy had the same kiddie carrier with a child on board that was excited and mesmerised by the fast-moving world around them and as we passed, we did a Dad to Dad nod. That universal single swift raise of the head that blokes do; a simple nod of acknowledgement, a nod of 'hey man we've got this' ... Then a moment later he did a double-take glance back. 'That wasn't a child ... was that a cask I saw ...?'

Up at Wray Castle we paused for a drink and a bite to eat. It was glorious sunshine so we'd emptied our water bottles pretty quickly. I headed off in search of more refreshment and returned with two slabs of the most divine ginger flapjack that I have ever tasted. Now I'm not usually a fan of flapjack – it's handy for cramming in a few calories but I'd never eat it for pleasure – but this was superb. It was covered in chocolate, riddled with ginger, and had a layer of cornflakes on top, if logistics had allowed it I would gladly have bought several kilos to keep us going over the coming days.

I, on the other hand, am the world's biggest fan of flapjack, and have to agree that despite its non-regulation layer of cornflakes, it was indeed and excellent flapjack.

We journeyed on towards Ambleside. Along the way we passed an older gentleman out walking with his son and while Steve chatted to the gent, I paused and had a natter with his son and asked how he was enjoying his walk.

'We're currently five hours into a two-hour walk,' he smiled. 'I hope you two aren't in a rush.'

'Well, we are running a little late.'

'Good luck with that. Dad swears he doesn't drink and just downed two pints of cider with his lunch. He could be there for hours.'

After a few more minutes 'dad' made a generous contribution to our collecting tins and we continued on our way. It's a narrow, winding route over into Ambleside but easy enough to follow and not too taxing – lots of hills to make you go 'weeee' and very few to make you go 'arrrghhh!'

I like to think I was channelling my inner Danny MacAskill as I ducked and weaved along the winding track, listening to the stones and gravel popping under the tyres. It was another baking hot day and although the track along Windermere had been largely under the shade of the trees, this stretch was more out in the open, but I found that if I kept up a decent pace the breeze kept me a bit cooler – so cool in fact that I

Wray Castle

didn't notice that I'd caught the sun until later that evening. I'd been too distracted setting up the cask on the kiddie carrier that I'd forgotten to put on sun cream. Ouch.

After rendezvousing with Grizedale Bikes and exchanging out bikes for rucksacks, we headed off to meet with Andrew from Fell Brewery. Little did I know it, but we were about to get a BIG lesson in brewing …

'Beer's not like gin, is it?' I ventured, fairly confidently. 'I mean, there's only four things in beer isn't there, it can't be that complicated, can it?'

Oh, how wrong I was …

Fell Brewery launched in 2013 with Tim as head brewer and Andrew looking after business, sales and marketing etc. They grew up in the Lake District and have known each other since school days. Having both gone their separate ways to university – Andrew to Manchester to study Molecular Cell Biology and Tim to Edinburgh to study Chemical Engineering – they remained in touch when they entered working life and both quickly realised that they weren't exactly loving the daily grind.

Following a three-week road trip across the USA, where they discovered that despite its reputation for weak, mass produced, lager, America was actually at the heart of the craft beer boom, they decided to take a crack at brewing their own. At this point, as Andrew puts it, they had 'No money and no knowledge, we just wanted to make beer!'

While Tim disappeared off to gain his MSc in Brewing and Distilling, Andrew got busy sorting out EU grants and premises. Now they knew lots about making beer but realised they had a lot to learn how to turn their dream into a commercially viable reality.

Stunning Windermere

They found their niche making new school beers that are sympathetic to the local market and quickly built up a strong local following and a reputation for producing unusual, but top quality, beers. They took time visiting all the 'cool' craft bars across the north of England and learned about consumer tastes and what might work, then focused all their energies on producing a distinctive range of beers.

Their team has grown around them and are generally trusted friends and ex-colleagues who they have known for a while, and they are quite open to any of their staff coming up with an idea for a new brew. When we met Andrew told us how they were currently experimenting with a recipe idea dreamed up by their delivery driver.

Given their scientific backgrounds, their approach to making beer is different from anyone else's we encountered, and Andrew has a gloriously geek-like love for yeast and loves tinkering with different varieties, including using naturally occurring yeast in some brews.

> I'd never really thought about the importance of the yeast, or how it could affect the brewing process; probably explains why my many attempts at cider have failed. How does one stop me cider double-fermenting and turning into pure spirit? Anyone?

> Andrew clearly loved the stuff and seemed to know an alarming amount about it.

We encountered their beers at a number of bars during our hike and they often surprised us, but they never disappointed. They also have a climbing wall in their brewery as they are all keen climbers apparently, but sadly had to take out the overhang section when they installed their new state of the art brewing kit. If you're after a beer that's definitely different, then these are certainly the guys to try.

Our heads spinning with our newly gained beer knowledge we set off in search of Ambleside Youth Hostel which was, refreshingly, in Ambleside. They are in a superb location, right at the head of the lake and we wandered off to the local chippy for tea. The problem was that the prices were nearly double what we'd pay at home, plus they didn't look all that amazing.

> I always go and get our chippy tea on Fridays. Beth is not a creature of habit apart from her Friday chippy tea, which she loves. I know exactly how much our chippy tea costs and was very glad when we agreed to

give this one a miss. Double the price? And the chips did not look good.
Neither did the sausage. Our local chippy gets them from the butchers
next door and they're lovely. These did not look lovely.

Ravenous, we walked back to the Youth Hostel where, it turns out, they have a fantastic cafe/restaurant where we enjoyed a huge plate of food and a well-earned pint of beer as we watched the sun set behind the Furness Fells.

Tomorrow was a big day with a big hill and, as I gazed at Loughrigg in the fading light, I tried not to think about how hard it would be hauling the cask up there. That was a worry for the morning.

As I drank my beer, I looked at Loughrigg. It looked big. Very big. Our first
proper fell. How would we do? The forecast was for another scorching
day; we chatted about the route and looked at some alternative options.
The problem is that until someone puts a chair lift in, there's no easy way
to the top.

The hostel was rammed with school parties having a fine old time and, while I absolutely applaud anything that gets kids stuck into the outdoors, I wasn't 100 per cent convinced that we'd be getting a great

The view from Ambleside Youth Hostel, the Furness fells bathed in the light of the setting sun

night's sleep – certainly not if they were anything like the school trips I'd been on as a teenager.

We turned in early, as did the kids. We turned the lights out and tried to get some sleep; they did not. The shouting, laughing and stampeding (seriously, what were they up to?) continued until bang on 11pm when a teacher went in and bellowed at them all to settle down and shut up. I smiled as I remembered the many school trips on which I'd misbehaved. Peace descended and we finally dozed off, with nothing but an owl outside the window disturbing the quiet of the night.

BREWERY: Fell Brewery

WEBSITE: www.fellbrewery.co.uk

BEERS: Ghyll Golden Ale, Tinderbox IPA, Helles Lager

TOURS? Not at the moment

TAP ROOM? Two bars – Fell Bar Kendal and Fell Bar Penrith

STOCKED: Local shops & bars

Ambleside

Rydal

Rydal•Water

Grasmere

Grasmere Brewery

Grasmere

An uphill struggle

- **Start**: Ambleside
- **End**: Grasmere
- **Distance**: 5 miles/ 8KM
- **Terrain**: Hard track and tarmac
- **Transportation**: Bus – 555 or 599

I THINK BEFORE WE GET STUCK into this chapter I need to give a bit of an overview of where the world was at this particular moment in time. We did our walk during late June/early July 2019 when Theresa May was still Prime Minister and the 'will we/won't we' Brexit debate was in full flow. Political tensions across the country were sky high so it seemed the perfect time to kidnap our local MP Tim Farron and drag him over Loughrigg with a beer cask.

We didn't rope him in for his political ideology, we roped him in because he's a thoroughly nice bloke who does a huge amount to support local causes and, like most folks, he enjoys a good pint at the end of a long hike.

As we were to be spending the entire day with Tim Farron I wanted to make sure that Casky was fully secured. The last thing we needed were headlines screaming 'Local MP crushed by rogue beer cask as perplexing hiking escapade goes badly wrong'. I checked and double checked the straps just to be absolutely certain.

When we first approached him about walking with us it was January 2019 and the Brexit leave date was 31 March 2019. As our plans progressed, so did the Brexit shenanigans and, at one point, the leave date was set for 30 June. I have to confess that when I heard that my heart sank, not for any political reasons but because it would have meant we'd be very unlikely to see Tim on top of Loughrigg on 27 June.

Flat calm on the morning of the trek up Loughrigg

Fortunately the date was then pushed back again to 31 October and, while the nation argued about whether or not this was a good thing, I breathed a huge sigh of relief because it meant we were in the clear for the walk again.

Tim is a Preston lad and, as he put it, 'Given where I was born, I ought to have been a "North-Ender", but having cousins in Darwen meant that I was lured into supporting Blackburn Rovers.' As an ardent Rovers fan, in 1991, he was at the FA Cup 3rd round match on 5 January when Blackburn Rovers played Liverpool. Rovers were leading right up to the 90th minute when Liverpool scored an equaliser which led to a rematch that put Blackburn out of the cup. Why is this important? Well, it's said that Wainwright, also a 'dyed in the wool' Blackburn Rovers fan (and founder member of the Blackburn Rovers Supporters Club), watched the match from his hospital bed and that the nail biting climax and subsequent disappointment were all too much. He sadly passed away on 20 January that year.

As a child Tim spent many of his weekends exploring the Lake District but it wasn't until after he won his first election that he discovered his passion for fell running. Prior to that he'd been a keen footballer but, once elected, was unable to commit to regular practice sessions, so he pulled on his running shoes instead.

I'm not quite sure what I expected from being with him for the day but I was surprised at how very little we talked about politics, even if the rest of the country could talk of nothing else. What struck me was that when we did talk about anything to do with his political career his focus always seemed to be on his desire to help people and he clearly enjoyed being able to make a positive difference in people's lives.

Our original plan had been to head up Nanny Brow because it's quieter and the views are pretty but, because it was so hot, we opted for the popular slog up from Rothay Park. We were beginning to get the measure of the cask and had very quickly discovered that tarmac was best and, even then, those that know the steep climb up the first stretch of Loughrigg, will understand the challenges we faced.

This was our first fell and it was a steep learning curve in every sense of the word. It was a glorious sunny still morning, lathered up on sun-cream and put a long sleeved top on – lesson learned from yesterday. Today was going to be the cask's first ever expedition traversing the higher fell terrain. How would the wheels hold up? It was a perfect test run for Helvellyn.

The first road section at Rothay Park may be easy tarmac terrain but is particularly steep so the cask had a gravitational pull back down to Ambleside.

With Tim Farron MP, our fellow cask hauler for the day

As we headed up and out into the open fell of Loughrigg, the path became rockier. This is where I became aware that Casky had a tipping point as it rolled over several times. I steadied the cask using both arms. Note to self, be aware of paths with drops, don't want it cask-cading down fellsides, that would be embarrassing, not to mention rather dangerous to those below.

Walking with a well-known face was certainly interesting; on the down side it meant that we had to stop a lot and it slowed us down but, on the plus side, it meant that we had to stop a lot so we could have a rest and a drink. Tim chatted amiably with absolutely everyone we met. I would say that he more than pulled his weight with the beer cask, but that would do him a disservice – it was hard to wrestle it from his grip, even though there wasn't a cloud in the sky and the thermometer was nudging towards 30C.

We renamed the cask Tim Gallon in his honour. It seemed the least we could do.

By the half way point Steve and Tim were working together like a well-oiled machine while I hung back answering lots of 'yes, that *is* who you think it is' queries.

There was a lot of lifting and carrying once we got off the top of the tarmac section. It wasn't easy getting it up and over some of the rockier sections, but it did make for some good photos.

A trig well conquered

The view from the top

Up at the trig point we attracted quite a crowd, which was great as many of them were happy to put money in our collecting tins. I also got chatting to a couple who were up there on honeymoon having only been married a few days before. I promised that I'd immortalise them in the book, but now I realise that I have no way to tell them that ... So, if anyone knows Nina and Laurie Kavanagh from Nottingham, who got married in late June 2019 and honeymooned in the Lake District, tell them I said hi!

As we made our way downhill we quickly discovered that down is only marginally less challenging than up when it comes to the beer cask – although it significantly faster.

Coming down the terrace steps had to be a mixture of pulling it from behind or as the steps became higher, manoeuvring forwards and gently lowering it down as not to damage the cask or make an annoying banging and clanging all the way down that would have been heard down the length of Grasmere valley.

With our new friends Nina and Laurie

Though most locals probably would have dismissed it as the sonic boom from a jet, racing through the valley.

As we descended towards Grasmere Tim chatted about his wife and children and even treated us to some funny stories about his Granny, who had been born in 1880 and, despite having taken the pledge in her twenties, had a bedside cabinet that remained swathed in the aroma of gin many decades after her death. We also discovered that he has a surprisingly punk/new wave taste in music and is a massive fan of Prefab Sprout.

I hadn't anticipated down being as tricky as it was. There's no braking system on the trolley and once it builds some momentum, it can be hard to stop. After a while I began to get the hang of it, something Beth never quite mastered and she swore at poor old Casky a lot more than I did. I like to think we developed an understanding – because I spent more time pulling I was more aware of when it was about to tip, or pull off to one side, so could take action before it went badly wrong. Beth ended up in the bracken rather more often.

When we finally arrived into Grasmere we headed directly for The Good Sport for a round of beers. The bar is the 'tap' room for Grasmere Brewery which is situated about 200 yards away so, as beer miles go, these guys are pretty green.

The brewery is owned and run by Paul and Beth and, out of everyone we met, these guys really stuck in my mind for their wonderful 'get

Cheers!

stuck in' approach – so much so that they reminded me a lot of Tom and Barbara Goode in The Good Life. Paul and Beth left the corporate world behind to launch into the world of brewing and now run a B&B as well as the pub and brewery.

When I say 'hands on' I really mean it. As Paul said 'Everything needs to be simple enough to fix ourselves,' and they do precisely that. Working on a budget they have slaved away to create miracles by converting a very run-down old weaving barn into a brewery. The land had been derelict for around fifteen years so was incredibly overgrown – their solution was to put pigs onto the land for eighteen months to dig up and eat all the roots. They started with one pig and, at one stage had as many as fifteen but they did have the occasional problem with escapees.

In amogst the action at Grasmere Brewery

I had visions of Last of the Summer Wine type escapades as a wild pig ran amok around Grasmere. When we first moved into our house our cat took off for two weeks. When we were out looking for him (he eventually sauntered home none the worse for his ordeal) we got to know the neighbours pretty well, and I should imagine an escaped pig would have a similar, if rather more memorable, effect.

In 2017 they turned their attention to beer, driven simply by a love for the drink. This was to be a common theme with the brewers we met – none of them saw it as a 'job', but rather a passion that they had followed. They talked to people and read stories of other brewers' experiences, which led them to buy the cafe at the end of the road and convert it into their tap room because that way they'd always at least have one customer.

For now at least they plan to keep everything small and brew small batches of fine tasting beers, with the occasional eccentric brew thrown in. They are happy to get creative with their brews and sometimes have to – Paul pointed out that if the big breweries decide that a particular variety of hops is fashionable the price rockets and it sells out fast. So, smaller breweries, like Grasmere, need to be flexible and creative and able to work with a wider variety of hops which, for folks who like tinkering with beer, is a lot of fun, but also presents problems with consistency. They've also experimented with cloudy beers – clear beer only really became a thing when we all started drinking out of nice clean glasses, before then, when folks drank from pewter tankards, clarity wasn't really an issue.

A colourful trio at Grasmere

The guys in Grasmere also make cider, specifically they make an apple cider which tastes lethal but isn't and a rhubarb cider which tastes like Fanta but will flatten you after one pint. Don't say I didn't warn you.

Don't let Beth near the rhubarb cider. Seriously. This is not a good idea. I've seen what she's like on cider. She knocks it back like fruit juice then wonders why she can't walk the next day. She tries to blame it on something she's eaten, but we all know the truth. Keeping her away from the cider was now my mission. We had a big swim and a lot of miles still ahead of us.

They were also the only folks we met who bottle their own beers having bought a broken-down bottling machine and figuring out how to fix it. They've got plans for canning too. In fact I wouldn't put anything past these folks; with their creativity and ingenuity nothing they do in the future would surprise me in the slightest.

Beers safely drunk it was time to get Tim back to his car in Ambleside. When we'd originally invited him, I'd offered to pay for a taxi to get him back, but he was having none of it and insisted on taking the bus. I offered bus fare but that was refused too. He disappeared outside to the bus stop and returned a few minutes later grinning.

'There's a bus in ten minutes,' he said, smiling from ear to ear. 'And it's the 599 – the open top one so I can sit upstairs.'

In an era of cynicism, when many of us have little faith in whatever is going on in Westminster, I thought it was rather lovely to see him smile at such a simple pleasure. I mean, who doesn't want to sit upstairs on an open top bus in the sunshine?

Having waved Tim off we plodded off to our accommodation; a 'bunk house' on the edge of town. We weren't expecting much but were mightily surprised to have a crisp, clear, sunny room in a beautiful quiet location.

Having done the obligatory washing of pants, socks and t-shirts in the sink we sat outside in the evening sunshine, guzzling tea (I was still very dehydrated), scoffing huge plates of pizza and pondering how on earth we were going to float the cask along Rydal water the next day ...

As we were doing our daily social media updates, we were thinking of all the different uses for the cask; a seat, bedside table, bike rack. Unsworth's suggested holding beer would be a novel idea. The very thought! It was still hot, 22°C and from the B&B we could see the first part of the route up towards Helvellyn. Was that going to be a step too far? Don't think about it. It'll be a nice swim on Rydal Water tomorrow, assuming it floats.

BREWERY: Grasmere Brewery

WEBSITE: grasmerebrewery.com

BEERS: Pale Ale, Stout, Bitter, Rhubarb Cider

TOURS? Not at present

TAP ROOM? The Good Sport in Grasmere

STOCKED: Local small shops & bars

Rydal

Rydal Water

Grasmere

Grasmere

Water ridiculous idea

- **Start**: North end of Rydal Water
- **End**: South end of Rydal Water – in The Badger Bar
- **Distance**: 1 mile/ 1.6KM
- **Terrain**: Water
- **Transportation**: Bus – 555 or 599

'AT LEAST YOU'VE GOT GOOD WEATHER' was the comment from pretty much everyone we chatted to along the way. Well, anyone who wasn't a hiker, that is. Yes, the weather was undeniably superb and decidedly un-English; temperatures across the country were racing past 30°C and, over in Paris, they'd just recorded their hottest temperature on record at 45.9°C. These may be perfect conditions for sun worshippers and long lazy evenings in the garden, but they were far from perfect conditions for long distance hikes, especially when accompanied by a beer cask.

We had the same problem when we got married back in August 2003 – the week before had seen the hottest temperatures on record. We must have been the only couple hoping the weather would get worse for our wedding day. Thankfully it did cool down a bit, but we still got to enjoy some sunshine. We weren't hauling a cask around then though – but I did have to wear a tail coat.

It wasn't just the hiking that was the problem; our budget was tight as it was, and certainly didn't stretch to air-conditioned rooms, so sleeping was also a major problem. Despite some lovely accommodation (and Thorney How really was a great place to stay) we were struggling to get

Stretching the trolley wheels in dappled sunshine before the big swim!

enough rest and were both waking up tired and tetchy.

Luckily, today we were swimming rather than hiking, but the hot conditions meant that our 12 noon departure time had been brought forward to 10am, so we dragged ourselves out of bed nice and early and enjoyed breakfast in the cool shade of the kitchen – it was already too hot for us to sit out in the sunshine.

It was a good couple of miles to our start point so we began slowly making our way down through the village. Our accommodation for that night had agreed that we could drop off our rucksacks just after breakfast to make things a bit easier.

Today we were fudging the route a little bit to be honest; we'd ideally have liked to come down off Loughrigg and stay in Rydal, then swim up Rydal Water and continue on foot into Grasmere. Two things had foiled our cunning plan; firstly we couldn't find any accommodation that we could afford in Rydal and secondly Suzanna, our swimming guide for the day, told us that we'd be swimming against the current, which for two novices was far from ideal. So we'd opted for two nights in Grasmere and a spot of route fudging.

As we wandered down to our meeting point we paused in the shade of the woods to munch a couple of Belvita biscuits and ponder what we were getting into. Although we were both swimmers and had swum out in the lakes several times, we'd never swum the entire length of a lake and certainly never towed anything before. We crunched our biscuits in introspective silence.

A perfect buoyancy aid

By the time we reached Suzanna she was well into getting everything prepared for us. As we squeezed ourselves into our wetsuits (kindly provided by Suzanna) we chatted about our mission; she told us we'd swim down the lake then get out by the Badger Bar for a pint. Bugger. We'd both been so focused on the swim that we'd left our wallets with our rucksacks. I did have my phone though so sent the bar a private message to see if we could sort out a couple of drinks and pay for them later ...

Caskimedes

The moment of truth, would Archimedes bathtub discovery hold water ... or indeed displace water?

Phew... it does float

> *For ours and Caskimedes' health and safety we needed buoyancy aids so as they were being blown up I took the cask into the water to test how well it floated and to get some photos. Eureka! It floated. It was a little top heavy at the handles but floated none the less.*

Down at the lake shore we inflated the floatation aids for the cask, even though Peter back at Unsworth's Brewery (who loaned us the cask) had pointed out that if the cask sank then the laws of physics would have failed and every boat in the world would sink too. I'm not one to question the laws of physics, but I figured that if the cask didn't need the additional floats then I might, so it was definitely best to take them.

As we set off along the river towards the lake Steve became convinced that there were crocodiles lurking in the reeds.

> *Well, with branches hanging low into the river it did look like the Amazon mangroves. I'm convinced I saw eyes peeking out of the water; ok it may have been water droplets on my glasses*

It turns out there were no crocodiles, or alligators (obviously) but there was a feisty swan, well known for taking a dislike to swimmers, but luckily he was off in the distance. We splashed onwards ...

No harm in a little help though

It's fair to say that our progress was slow. Magnificently slow. Some may even describe it as glacial. (I prefer the term 'regally slow'.) It had nothing to do with the cask (which Suzanna towed most of the way muttering things about risk assessment and health and safety) and everything to do with me and Steve not being fast swimmers.

The length of time it took us to swim the length of Rydal, a couple of jet planes had flown over a few times, probably having done laps of the Lake District. I think only to come back just to get another glance, yup that was a cask those swimmers were swimming with … To be honest it was a lovely hot day and I was just enjoying a relaxing swim.

I used the time to chat to Suzanna about precisely how she'd ended up as a swimming guide. Like me she hailed from the West Midlands, in her case growing up in Coventry, where, when I visited as a kid, my biggest treat was a swim in the Olympic sized swimming pool. I wondered if I'd ever seen her there?

'No, I was a proper suburban kid, not really into the outdoors at all.'

'So, how did all this happen then?'

Her journey north began when some friends of the family bought a place near Skiddaw which needed doing up. On one occasion

Definitely no crocodiles here

Suzanna accompanied her dad when he came up to help with a spot of redecorating. She remembers looking out of the window at Skiddaw and simply thinking 'wow'.

Suzanna is forthright, headstrong and certainly not the sort of person to sit on her heels and watch as life drifts by, so she got herself a housekeeping job, moved up and found a nice house to share. She walked a little, took the odd dip in the lakes on hot days but nothing more. But, it turned out, her housemate was a very keen swimmer and would head out at 6am most days for a dip. As Suzanna puts it: 'The house was lovely, but old, and it was impossible to leave quietly; everything rattled, so every morning she woke me up. One day I thought, "If you can't beat them, join them" and went out for an early morning swim with her, and I've been hooked ever since.'

As she did more swims she looked into getting qualified to lead swims, but there were no specific swimming guide qualifications on the market at that time, so she got herself qualified in swift water rescue, open water lifeguarding etc., which taught her how to weigh up the risks. It was clear from our time with her that safety is her paramount concern.

As Beth and Suzanna chatted, I drifted along quite happily in the sunshine. I was enjoying the views and keeping an eye out for crocodiles …

These days she offers a range of guided swims throughout the year, some as part of groups, others as a personal guide, but she's adamant that you don't have to be a top swimmer to enjoy open water swimming; 'Sometimes all people need is a bit of confidence and they see me as a sort of "portable lifeguard".' Makes perfect sense.

By now we'd eventually made it to the end of the lake, having set a new slow record of well over 90 minutes. We were just pleased to have made it. As we pulled off our suits Suzanna offered lots more useful bits of advice about how to look after cuts etc. following an open water swim. I took the chance to examine the cask and was delighted to see that the stickers that we'd been collecting along the way had all survived intact.

Finally at the Badger Bar they were kind enough to allow us to get a round of beers and crisps and pay for them later. I really want to tell you what we drank, and I know I should have taken a photo, but we were utterly exhausted and I was barely thinking straight. I remember there

Who said 'crocodiles'?!

was beer and crisps and that's about it; I'm pretty sure travel writers are meant to remember more than that. I made a mental note to do better in future, but I immediately forgot that too.

Bidding Suzanna farewell we plodded back into Grasmere and crashed out on the bed for an hour or so. It was hot. Very hot. Tomorrow was likely to be hotter and tomorrow we were meant to be hauling the cask up Helvellyn. I know we were both worried, but we tried not to think about it. Then we did think about it. Perhaps we could persuade other folks to join us to make carrying the cask a bit easier? Between them, the cask and trolley weighed 24KG, and that was on top of our huge backpacks.

We returned to The Good Sport for food and, although the food was fabulous, we were both too exhausted and stressed to properly enjoy it. We each ate a few mouthfuls and pushed the rest around the plate. We checked Twitter to see if anyone could come and help but no-one could. It was just us. We checked our maps and plotted a Plan B route through the woods alongside Thirlmere in case we couldn't face the summit. To be honest, at the precise moment in time I doubted whether I could even manage that. We both felt utterly drained.

We found that the heat hadn't helped in many respects, with eating, drinking, sleeping, and walking, with a cask in tow. Mind you I don't think

How high?

rain would have been better. I needed my strength – I knew Beth had a dodgy back so I'd be doing the majority of the pulling, and this wasn't just any fell, this was Helvellyn – 950m high and the third highest fell in the county.

I tried to pick a filling dish with plenty of carbohydrates that would give me the energy required. Unfortunately, it was simply too heavy, and my stomach refused to listen to reason and was not having a good feed no matter what. I stopped forcing it down, worried that it may try and make a break for freedom again. This might have been a beer hike, but I was not really having all that much beer at all, neither was Beth (I don't think I've ever seen anything put her off a beer before!) I tried a thirst-quenching pint of light ale but couldn't even manage that. Desperate for something to drink, I managed to glug some water before we left.

As Steve headed back to the B&B, I picked up some snacks for our hike from the Co-op; whatever our route we were going to be leaving very early to try and beat the heat and would be gone before breakfast was being served. It was still hot and muggy outside and I may have lingered a little longer that was necessary in the nice, cool, air-conditioned, Co-op.

Back at the B&B, the room was lovely but the heat stifling. Tired, sticky and despondent we turned off the light and tried to get some sleep.

Legburthwaite

Thirlmere

Helvellyn

Red Tarn

Dollywaggon Pike

Grisedale Tarn

Grasmere

Up

- **Start**: Grasmere
- **End**: Legburthwaite
- **Distance**: 8 miles/ 13KM
- **Terrain**: Tarmac and hard track
- **Transportation**: Bus – 555 and 599

TODAY WE HAD BEEN DUE to walk with friend, and author, Mark Richards. Mark had walked with Wainwright and draws wonderful pen and ink line drawings to accompany his many walking guides. Regardless of the weather, we'd selected our companion for the day very carefully; even when we were planning we knew that today we needed someone with us who knew what they were doing in the fells. We knew that we'd have enough on our hands manhandling a beer cask to the top of Helvellyn without having to keep an eye on a novice hiker, so we had been very careful about who we'd selected.

A week or so prior to the hike I'd had a message exchange with Mark which went something like this:

Mark: 'Do you mind if I bring a friend with me on the hike?'

Me: 'Can they haul a trolley with a beer cask strapped to it?'

Mark: 'Yes!'

Me: 'In that case you can bring whoever you want.'

We had no idea who the someone else was, but I'd figured the more the merrier; many hands make light work, and all that.

Around 5:30am I gave up the sweaty pretence of sleep and switched on the phone. There was a message from Mark's wife informing us that Mark had been up all night with massive toothache and the only thing he'd be doing that day was visiting the emergency dentist. I was reassured, however, that his friend, now our sole walking companion for the day, Jeanette Moore, would still be coming and would meet us outside the Co-op as arranged.

Steve stirred. He's not a morning person but even he couldn't manage a lie in in this heat. I told him of the development. We chatted for a while before agreeing that much as we'd love to get the cask to the top of Helvellyn, at this stage it really was no longer an option. It was baking hot, we were already exhausted and now our only walking companion was someone whose abilities in the fells we were unaware of. I made breakfast and we told our followers across social media that although the hike was on, the walk to the top of Helvellyn most definitely was not.

I sighed, it was already sunny. I was so annoyed, with myself and with the weather. I really wanted to do this. I kept mulling over the scenarios while Beth made people aware of our plans. But we could try it; I wasn't giving up just yet.

We set off to our rendezvous to meet Jeanette, who was already waiting for us. Once outside it struck us that it was nowhere near as hot as it had been and the sky was, for the first time in days, covered in cloud.

It's clouded up, hmmm ...

Jeanette, it turns out, is half woman half mountain goat, and the perfect companion for a high fell adventure. We told her of our change in route plans and studied the map together so we all knew what was going on.

I walked behind with the cask, looking at the clouds, at our distant route meandering swiftly up towards and around the crags of Seat Sandal. But it's just there ...

This traveller needs some rest...

As we made our way out of the village we chatted politely as we got to know each other. Jeanette had, most recently, had been director of a charity, before in January 2019 deciding to give full-time writing a go. She'd already produced one volume of short stories (*Rucksack Tales*), had completed one novel and had another well underway. She's also a regular contributor to the magazine produced by Keswick retailer George Fisher. I was too busy talking about writing with Jeanette to notice Steve's change of mood.

We approached the point where we would have turned off if we'd been going up Helvellyn. I looked and Steve and suddenly noticed a gleam in his eye. My heart sank a little as I realised what this meant.

'It's a lot cooler than yesterday,' he ventured.

'But we are both exhausted, and it's a flipping long way,' I replied.

He was prodding his phone, looking at the map then looking up the track towards Helvellyn. As we stood there a van drove past beeping its horn, the driver waving wildly through the window. We waved back, discovering later that it was someone who'd been following our adventures on social media.

'Well?' I asked.

Just then a fell runner appeared at the top of the track heading towards us.

'We'll ask him what the track's like,' said Steve. The runner approached, Steve asked him what the track was like.

'I wouldn't try hauling that up there,' came the reply.

I groaned. From that point on I knew exactly where we were heading. Up.

Oh yeah!
Kaggi.

The cask now needed a name for this adventure. Seeing as Helvellyn could be translated to Old Norse origins, an

That Steve is such
a slave-driver

It started off hilly and bumpy

Old Norse name was in order. How about Aegir, a giant sea lord as well as a brewer; a commander of the waves and the foam of the beer. The brewer to the Gods no less, so must have been pretty good at brewing a decent pint.

In the end I decided on Kaggi, Old Norse for keg or cask.

Jeanette had struck me as a very sensible hill walker. When we first met, she'd asked questions about what time, and where, we planned to stop for lunch. We never know the answer to that question on the best of days, and we certainly didn't know it today. And on top of that, here we were, completely changing our route on a whim. To her eternal credit she just went along with it, and we began making our way up the track.

It is tricky saying how long it takes to hike somewhere in the fells, too many variables, especially when walking with someone you don't know, you have no idea how fast they will walk. One thing we had yet to correctly factor in was 'Cask Time'. Not only time to stop and chat to hikers, but also time to deal with terrain obstacles. We both, our walking guests and us, hadn't anticipated or planned how long it would take for each day's adventure. This time I made it clear, I would be getting this cask up Helvellyn no matter how long it took. We would get there when we got there. Luckily Jeanette was ok with that.

It wasn't too bad to begin with; we bumped along, steadily gaining height and dodging fell runners who continued to trickle down past us. When the route forked we took the route along Little Tongue Gill, taking it in turns to haul the cask, although Steve was still doing the lion's share.

Caption competition, anyone?

I managed to get another clegg bite – it wasn't an issue that day but it was going to cause problems a day or so later.

Both being writers, me and Jeanette had plenty to natter about as we plodded upwards. Jeanette released a book of short stories (*Rucksack Tales*, as J. M. Moore), all set in the Lake District, and is wholeheartedly following her passion to become a full-time writer.

Making our way along Hause Riggs we were passed by a group of Danish hikers; it was hard enough explaining what we were doing, and why, to everyone, without a language barrier getting in the way. We must have done ok though as they all put a donation in our pot.

'Tak!' I smiled, feeling quite chuffed that I'd remembered how to say 'thanks' in Danish. They all smiled back, before continuing onwards chatting in their Mother Tongue. If I'd listened more closely perhaps I could have added the phrase 'lunatic English people' to my Danish vocabulary.

Meanwhile I gazed down the valley 'I guess we should have taken the path to the right ...' I was looking down at the perfectly good track that led up Tongue Gill to Hause Gap.

'That steady path up there?' quizzed Jeanette in a polite yet underlying 'Are you kidding me?!' kind of way. Well, all routes have their swings and roundabouts, their bouncy rocky tracks and their steep vertigo inducing 'make sure the cask is secure I'm not running down after it' grassy hillsides.

We tried keeping out of the way of the fell runners as much as we could, but many of them not only stopped to talk to us, but also put generous donations into our collecting tins. The first wave were on a 100km run and had started out at midnight.

Some had heard about what we were doing 'Ah it's the famous cask!' came jolly responses from mud splattered ultra runners as they sprinted past.

'You'll meet the sprint guys higher up,' one of them said. 'They just started out from Glenridding and are only doing 50km.' Yeah, I always sprint when it's just 50km up a mountain ...

We made it to Grizedale Tarn where we collapsed in a heap for lunch. I noticed that all three of us had sat with our backs to Dollywaggon

They must be mad! Oh, hang on...

Pike, the very worst part of the hike, looming large behind us. We ate, we nattered, we drank and then we realised that we could put it off no longer. More 'up' was required.

I have to be completely honest here and say that, due to a bad back, I was not a lot of use at carrying the cask and trolley on the whole of this hike. Thankfully Jeanette was and, as I watched her getting stuck in without a murmur of a grumble, I couldn't help thinking how we'd

Grizedale Tarn

struck lucky. She gladly pitched in as we all grew more and more tired towards the top. I joined in the rotation of cask hauling and we did what we could in short bursts. The bursts got shorter and shorter as we got more and more tired until, at one stage, we were doing ten paces then resting. We were all yawning fit to burst and were all desperately tired.

As the path zigzagged up, I had to hold the handle with both hands as I tried to steer around the larger rocks and over the smaller ones, trying not to scratch and dent Kaggi too much. The wellbeing of Kaggi was important and he had a tipping point. Often I felt him go over the 45 degree angle and race down the hillside to join the fell runners. Like an excitable terrier pulling at the lead, free, bounding down across the fells.

When it rolled over, it went fast so I had to grip hard to tame it, to keep it under control. I didn't fancy chasing after it, or having to drag it all the way back up again. I would have done though, if I'd had to, there was no way I was going to give up now.

As the rocks became larger, and the drains across the track more numerous, Jeanette helped by lifting up the other end to make traversing a little easier. It made a big difference.

All I wanted was a sit down and have a decent rest, but Steve insisted we kept pushing on to 'the post'; an old metal post at the top of the climb. I absolutely did not want to do that, I wanted to rest, but we all hung in together until, eventually, 'the post' appeared. Hallelujah! We all sank to the floor and drank whatever we could get our hands on. Jeanette threw £5 into our collecting pot and sank a bottle of IPA in a few gulps. We convinced ourselves it's precisely what our ancestors would have done.

From this side you can break Helvellyn into three parts; from the base to Grisedale Tarn, the steep path up to 'the Post' on the top of the western flanks of Dollywagon Pike and then the relative gentle walk to Helvellyn summit. The post is also a handy navigation point during those foggy treks to steer you clear of the craggy drops of the Eastern side.

By now, people who had passed us on their way up were heading back down and stopping for a natter or a few words of encouragement. We polished off all our water and the last of the beers from Bowness

Bay; our rucksacks were undeniably lighter, but we still had a long old way to go.

The route from the top of Dollywaggon to the summit of Helvellyn is very straightforward and, with our spirits revived and the summit in sight, we set off, still managing to have a few good laughs along the way.

Eventually, eight hours after leaving Grasmere, we made it! We were on top of Helvellyn with our beer cask. We were all utterly exhausted but over the moon. We posed for photographs, strangers gave us food and drink; we couldn't quite believe what we'd done. We all wanted to stay longer but reports were coming in that the weather was about to break and there was a risk of thunderstorms. Getting caught on top of Helvellyn in a thunderstorm would be unwise at the best of times, but it would be staggeringly unwise to be caught up there with a large aluminium beer cask and trolley.

Steve set off downhill with the cask at a pace which would have impressed Mo Farrah. Me and Jeanette plodded along behind, putting the world to rights and complaining about how many bits of the body

Whatever you do, don't let the cask roll down there...

Very proud moment

begin to misbehave as you get older. On our way down we passed a Lake District Three Peaks Group, trying to bag Helvellyn before the storm arrived; they told us to chat to their support crew in the car park and they'd give us a donation. We thanked them and continued plodding.

I wanted to get as many photos as I could of our achievement, while being mindful of the thunderstorm that was forecast. Being up in the fells, it's much easier to see the weather, particularly clouds of vertical rain, and in which direction they drift. I could see it raining stair rods over Coniston and heading north. Time to go.

To be honest, they didn't look like thunderclouds and though the trolley had big rubber tires I still didn't fancy being up high holding a metal cask by only a tube of 12mm foam pipe insulation. Gripping tensely, I felt cold metal against the middles of my fingers. I stopped, took out the reel of insulation tape from my backpack. I had been carrying all this extra weight with me 'just in case' so seemed a very good time to use it. The clue was in the name so I was reasonably confident that it was going to save me in the event of a lightning strike. I held the foam around the metal handle and reapplied a good dose of insulation tape.

Thinking about it, lightning is pretty hot, perhaps keeping my hands safe was the least of my worries. Or maybe I just needed more tape. Or different tape? Which was more resistant to heat? Maybe I should have got gaffer tape or was that duct tape?

I left Beth and Jeanette to natter as I jogged closely followed by a bouncing, clanking, cask. Even though Unsworth's were more concerned with the Kaggi's innards being in good working order, rather than his outward complexion, we had been careful in trying not to damage the cask in any way. It's possible he may have earned a few battle scars on the way down ...

I stopped to chat to one of the Cumbrian Three Peakers hiking up and some ten minutes later again as he came down after being informed on his radio to come back down, the storm was definitely coming.

I am really not a fan of down. When, one day, I eventually make my millions, I will not be paying for a helicopter to drop me off on the top of magnificent summits, oh no, I am quite happy to hike up to the top of said magnificent summit all by myself, but I will gladly pay for a helicopter to pick me up and bring me back down again. Down is relentless and I was spectacularly glad to reach the car park.

We found the Three Peaks support crew who not only gave us the promised donations, but also supplied us with much needed food and water; I'd packed provisions for our low level 'Plan B' route and was woefully under prepared for what we'd actually achieved. Still, we'd survived.

By now it was pouring with rain, thankfully no thunder, and we were on our way to the pub for a swift pint with Jeanette before she was whisked away by a friend and me and Steve trudged off to find our digs. When it came time to part there were huge hugs all round; we may have started the day as complete strangers but now we were firm friends.

Our accommodation for the night turned out to be the very worst we were to encounter on the entire hike. The camping barn was poorly signposted meaning we walked an additional half mile or so in the pouring rain. The landlady had clearly learned everything she knew about hospitality from old episodes of Fawlty Towers, and we cringed

A stony descent with the storm on our heels

as she yelled at a passing Duke of Edinburgh group and begrudgingly showed us to our beds.

There was a long list of rules pinned next to the door, one of them clearly stated 'NO BEER PARTIES'. Had she not noticed us pulling our own beer cask ...?

Ahead of the hike I'd contacted them and explained what we were doing and asked if we could drop our sleeping bags off beforehand and collect them afterwards. 'No problem,' they'd told me. 'In fact,' they'd added, without any prompting whatsoever from me, 'why don't we just let you have a couple of sleeping bag liners?' I'd thought how friendly and helpful they sounded. Now they were charging us £4 each for this kind offer.

There were fourteen beds in the 'barn' and only one toilet, in a breezeblocked-off corner and with a twelve- inch gap under the door. This led to a night of toilet visits with tactical coughing. The air was heavy with the scent of fourteen sweaty bodies crammed into a confined space during searing temperatures and with very few windows. On top of all that there were no power sockets in the 'barn', no hot water anywhere and showers were £1 each for ten minutes. I stunk. Steve stunk. But neither of us was in any mood to pay £1 for a shower.

We had arranged to meet our next walking companion at 8:30am the next morning; neither of us had been looking forward to an early start, but now it couldn't come soon enough. Alex, our companion for the next day, sent me a text to confirm everything.

'Do you want me to bring a couple of bacon rolls?' he asked.

'I think I love you,' I muttered.

'Love you too!' came Steve's voice from the top bunk. He need never know that this conversation was between me and a bacon roll.

Steve swept a pile of crumbs off his £4 sheets and we both sank down to get what sleep we could.

I think they were crumbs, out of all of the things they could be, crumbs would be a bonus. I peered at them more closely. At least they didn't crawl. Yeah, I think I'll sleep fully clothed and keep my hat on ...

The barn filled with whispered tones as the bedtime rituals began, always a joy to unavoidably catch a glimpse of someone in their nighty, scratching their backside as they barefooted to the toilet. After a while, the unmistakable glow of blue light filters pulsed behind closed curtains, gently lighting the exposed beams and slate roof. Then, one by one, the glows faded as their owners drifted off to sleep.

Legburthwaite

Keswick

Keswick Brewing Co.

Derwentwater

Best boot forwards!

- Start: Legburthwaite
- End: Keswick
- Distance: 5.5 miles/ 8.8KM
- Terrain: Tarmack, hard track, soft ground
- Transportation: Bus – 555 and 599

THE NEXT MORNING the musty barn was full of early morning whisperings as folks tried to get up and out without disturbing everyone else. That was one thing we'd noticed on our journey so far which turned out to be true for the rest of our hike; the cheaper the accommodation the more considerate the other guests. In the small B&Bs and Youth Hostels we found people to be, on the whole, considerate of others re noise etc. On the couple of occasions we had to stay somewhere smarter due to a lack of other available accommodation, the other guests were more prone to letting doors slam and talking loudly into the early hours with little thought for others.

Probably due to the previous day's excitement I think I got a reasonable night's sleep considering I was fully clothed and had a 5am wake-up call from our European bunk-bed neighbours.

We chatted to a couple of other guests as we drank coffee in the communal kitchen; they were visiting from London and, it turns out, were as unimpressed with the accommodation as we were. Somewhat mortified that this would be their impression of Cumbria we directed them to Thorney How for their next visit – very similar price, not a million miles away distance wise, but a world away when it came to the quality of accommodation offered.

Another one of the rules was the morning room inspection. I didn't fancy trying to explain the unidentified objects in my sheets nor did I want to pay for them in laundry bills. Dutifully though, not wanting to feel the wrath of the scary matron, I took off the sheets and duvet cover, as we had been instructed, and folded them neatly. Then I quickly left – bacon butties were calling!

My phone flashed; Alex had arrived with fresh, hot, bacon sandwiches. I raced outside and just about managed a polite 'hello' before shovelling it down my throat – he'd persuaded the lovely folks at Jan's Sandwich Shop to open early especially for us and, for that, I will be eternally grateful.

In between greedy mouthfuls we filled him in on the events of the previous day and the challenges of our camping barn and readied ourselves for the hike. Thankfully his wife (and business partner) Kerrie would be taking our rucksacks so we had a very much needed lighter walk. We had an important appointment with a large roast dinner in Keswick at 11:30am (yes, by this time in the hike, pretty much everything revolved around food!) so couldn't afford to hang around, so travelling light was a real boost.

We've known Alex and Kerrie for a while but, to be honest, didn't know all that much about them so this would be the perfect opportunity to learn more. Both of them are Cumbrian born and bred, Alex from

Alex, bringer of bacon

Across St John's in the Vale

Keswick and Kerrie from West Cumbria. Alex was born with a club foot and requires one 6 ½ shoe and one 8 ½ shoe; his parents always made sure he had good shoes but this was, obviously, never easy, which perhaps helps to explain why he now runs a very successful, multi-award-winning, walking boot shop.

Our route was a pretty straightforward six-miler into Keswick and, with no rucksacks and three of us sharing the hauling duties, things were looking good. We started off along St John's in the Vale before hopping up and over, past the church (and thankfully our only hill of the day) and on, down into Keswick. We've driven much of that route many, many, times, so it was lovely to walk it with a friend and take it all in.

Alex took charge of the cask again – result! We all tootled along, us assuming that because he lived not too far away Alex knew the route –

Moody mountains

St John's Church (it is in the vale as the name suggests)

and Alex, assuming we'd meticulously planned every step of the journey, placing his full trust in our navigational decisions. Despite all of that we didn't get too lost and only zigzagged across one boggy field.

When we arrived at the church we were all properly thirsty, and our trusty flasks were in our rucksacks with Kerrie. ('It's only a short walk,' I'd said. 'We won't need our flasks,' I'd said. Proof you really should

A bovine reception

never listen to me!) It was Sunday and people were arriving for the morning service, so I ventured inside seeking a little Christian hospitality and was rewarded with three cups and directions to the nearest tap; I wondered, for a moment, about enquiring if turning it into wine was still something they could do, but thought better of it. We sat on a bench in the churchyard, guzzling water and learning more about Alex.

Keswick Boot Company sprang into life in 2009 after Alex had risen as far as he could through the ranks of a major outdoor clothing chain and fancied a new challenge. Fortunately for them it was a really tough winter with sheet ice everywhere (which, in my knackered state I mis-heard as 'Sheeps Eyes' and wondered what they hell sort of business they'd been operating!). A harsh winter is something which may have proven a problem for many fledgling businesses, but Alex and Kerrie had the foresight to stock Yak Tracks (which clip to the bottom of your shoes and prevent you slipping over on the ice), and these sold like hot cakes and gave them the starting boost they needed.

Since then they have gone on to build a hugely popular and successful business in the heart of the town. They've amassed many thousands of followers across social media, won several awards and developed a rock-solid reputation for superb customer service. Alex knows only too well how tough it can be finding the right boots so takes all the time customers need to ensure they find the perfect fit.

We always get our boots from there and my favourite part is walking up and down the pretend hill. Oh, and looking at all the old boots they have on display. And picking out funky laces. Beth likes all the whisky bottles, although she usually prefers full ones.

Thirst slaked and midges descending, we returned our cups and continued our journey into Keswick, arriving just in time for our precious lunch appointment. The only fly in the ointment was that the clegg bite I'd acquired on Helvellyn was misbehaving badly and my arm was swelling up like

The Wainwright, Keswick

87

With John and Kate

Popeye. Steve was dispatched in search of Piriton and Anthisan, which he needed to retrieve from my rucksack in the back of Alex's car, while I chatted with John and Kate, owners of The Wainwright Pub and tried not to scratch my arm to bits.

If you've never been in there, The Wainwright is a proper pub with lots of wonderfully interesting bits and pieces around the walls and a huge commitment to supporting local brewers and suppliers. All of their beers (bar one, more of that shortly) are from Cumbrian breweries and we recognised many of the names from folks we'd either already met (Fell Brewery, Bowness Bay etc.) or those we were yet to see (Ennerdale, Keswick Brewery, etc.). They also serve wonderful home cooked meals and insist on all their food having total traceability so they know precisely where their meat, fish etc. comes from.

Steve returned clutching my meds and although I hated the drowsy feeling I always get from Piriton, my mottled arm dictated that I step up to a full dose. I swallowed my pills with a large swig of beer and hoped there were no 'no drinking' instructions on the leaflet I'd thrown away earlier in the hike to save on weight …

Honestly, she makes it sound so easy. First I had to find Alex, no mean feat because they were judging a dog contest at the town fete, then I had to find the car, again, not easy in Keswick on a sunny Sunday in June, and then I had to rummage through Beth's rucksack to find the pills and cream she was after. Any man who has ever had to rifle through his wife's handbag looking for something will sympathise.

'So, you must have some sort of background in pub management to take on a place like this,' I smiled, as I smeared antihistamine cream all over my arm.

'Nope, none at all,' John replied. 'We were sat in a pub garden one afternoon, chatting with a friend, drinking beer, when it came up that this pub was for sale. We were lucky enough to buy it and now, with

Who's for a pint?

the support of a great team in the pub and kitchen, the former "Four in Hand" is now thriving as "The Wainwright".'

It turns out that neither John nor Kate can pull a proper pint, but they have worked hard to create the sort of pub that they wanted to go to. They made a commitment early on to only stock Cumbrian beers but there's one notable exception.

'People would come in and ask for a pint of Wainwright, which we didn't stock on account of the fact it's brewed in Lancashire, not Cumbria.' Kate explained. 'When we didn't have it, rather than try one of the Cumbrian ales on offer, they'd just turn on their heels and leave, so we ended up stocking it.'

Even the art on the walls is from local artists and a map next to the bar shows the location of all the breweries in the county. This really is a proper 'local' in every single sense of the word.

John and Kate made sure we were topped up with fresh beers and then disappeared off to chat to other guests while we devoured two colossal roast dinners with all the trimmings.

That roast dinner was so good and so needed. It was finally a wee bit cooler and I finally felt like eating. I think it was the first full meal I could eat, and I ravenously wolfed it all down. I eyed Beth's Yorkshire pudding, but didn't fancy taking my chances. Her system was full of beer and Piriton. There was no telling what she could do.

A couple of groups at nearby tables had heard our conversation and made donations to our collecting tins; one guy had even been following us on Twitter and snapped a selfie with us – we felt like proper celebs!

After lunch we waddled out into the sunshine. 'Do we get a rest now?' asked Steve, hopefully.

'Erm, not exactly,' I replied. 'We still have one brewery and a gin shop to visit.'

He fixed me with his Paddington Bear hard stare.

'What? We need to cram in as much as we can. And anyway, next up it's Sue at Keswick Brewery and she's lovely!'

Mildly pacified we wandered over to see Sue, owner of Keswick Brewing Company and one of only two breweries we'd allowed into our gin book.

'Beer, or tea?' she asked as we arrived.

We were in the middle of a beer hike, carrying a beer cask and standing in one of the loveliest breweries in Cumbria. I looked at Beth wiling her to ask for tea. 'Tea please,' she said. Thank goodness! Turns out you can have too much of a good thing.

Since we last met things have been racing on for Sue and the brewery. When we were last here they had a small, but lovely, bar area and a good sized car park. Now they've renovated and expanded into an old outbuilding as well as building a large extension to create a light and airy bar and shop and much improved brewery tours. As well as their own beers they plan to feature guest beers in the tap room, which manages to be crisp and modern on the inside and still blend in perfectly with the traditional look of the neighbourhood from the outside.

Some of the impressive selection brewed by Keswick Brewing Company

As we enjoyed our huge mugs of tea Sue explained that to celebrate the new premises, they've redesigned all their pump clips and launched a new range of beers. From our previous visits we know that Sue is not one to stand still and is always creating new and exciting brews. She also produces 'Thirst Rescue' a popular local drink with 5p from every pint sold going directly to support Mountain Rescue.

The building work was still underway when we visited but there was enough completed to get a real feel for how it was all going to look and Sue's excitement was palpable. In an era of so much doom and gloom it's rather wonderful to see such a lovely local business bucking the trend and doing so well. We revisited in October 2019 for the opening to The Fox Tap and it really is a wonderful place to sit and enjoy a pint and it's great to see the place going from strength to strength.

Sue, being the wonderful woman that she is, tried her utmost to persuade us to take some beers away with us but we knew how heavy it made our rucksacks, so reluctantly declined.

'Are you off for a rest now?' she asked as we said our goodbyes.

'Not quite – just a quick stop at Sheepish before the B&B' I replied as we headed out onto the street.

I really did wish that I could just go and put my feet up, but I knew the guys at Sheepish (now known as the Wild Sheep Distillery) stocked an amazing array of local beers and had now ventured into gin production, so Beth definitely wanted to go and see what they were up to. Luckily it was only just around the corner from Sue's place. On our way we had to walk past Keswick Laundry and, I don't know why, but I always think that name would suit an upmarket/ trendy restaurant/ winebar. Maybe they could serve pints while you watched your washing. Has anyone ever even considered that possibility?

You always know if the Sheepish Shop is open as soon as you turn into the street because it's got a funky sheep in the window. Fair enough. James and Jo originally hail from t'other side of the Pennines but started selling their Sheepish branded clothing on Keswick market in 2010. In 2014 they decided they liked it so much that they'd stay and so they bought the shop, initially just selling clothing until a brewing friend suggested they try their hand at making beer.

We were deep in conversation when Sue from the brewery appeared at the door.

Us with James, Jo, and a flock load of alcohol!

'I know you can't carry beer,' she said 'but you must need cake.' And with that, she thrust two huge slabs of beer infused fruitcake into our hands before racing out again. You can see why I like Sue, can't you?

The Sheepish shop has an utterly unique feel and that's because it's not been created by a bland marketing company, every single inch of it has been built by James and Jo. They've recycled cable drums and other bits of wood and old fixtures and fittings to create something truly unique, and they've done it all without grants or funding, by continually re-investing in their business.

Yum!

Zzzzz...

Today they stock a range of beers alongside their wonderfully flavoured spirits (honestly, the salted caramel rum was an absolute revelation!) and, when we visited, the launch of their very first properly distilled gin was just a few weeks away. I was also getting distracted by their thoroughly unique range of handbags but, as Steve pointed out (quite rightly for once, he'd better not make a habit of it!) there was no way I could carry a cask, a rucksack and a handbag. I was all for giving it a go though! As I write this I've heard that they've halted their clothing line, hopefully temporarily, but the spirits are going from strength to strength. (You see what I did there?)

Seriously, I have to live with this.

By now I was dead on my feet. I had beer, tea, Piriton and salted caramel rum coursing through my veins and I just needed a lie down. We bid James and Jo a fond farewell, being in far too weakened a state to fight off the bottle of salted caramel rum being thrust into my hands, and made our way up to Alex to collect our rucksacks and head for Sunnyside Guesthouse and finally a bed for the night.

Nicky and Paul welcomed us with open arms and showed us to our room, and I did try to make polite conversation, honest I did, but all I could manage was a few pleasantries before I collapsed onto the bed. We did go out in search of food later on, but it didn't end well, so I'll let Steve tell you all about that.

Mind the bumps, Steve, I'm trying to have a snooze!

Why would you do that you know there won't be any grammar or punctuation or paragraphs when I go off on one of my monologue rants it doesn't play well with your grammar OCD?

Ok, it went something like this ... We went out for an early evening stroll around Keswick looking for something to eat all we wanted was something light like a sandwich in a cafe and there are loads of cafes and sandwich shops in Keswick but they were all closed and the ones that were open only did big meals not sandwiches so it seems the consumption of bread products are not allowed after lunchtime.

We both looked at each other and had a 'Falling Down' breakfast menu moment. (If you've not seen the film, Michael Douglas's character rather loses the plot after being a minute or so too late to order breakfast in a famous fast-food chain. That'll teach him to go into a fast-food chain instead of a local cafe, but I'm getting distracted again.) As it goes his wife was called Beth. Spooky, but don't worry we didn't go into full 'Falling Down' mode as the chippy was open, although it came close when it turned out they had no mushy peas.

Right. Rant over. Back to using punctuation again now.

To be honest, all I really remember are the cool, clean, white sheets ...

BREWERY: Keswick Brewing Company

WEBSITE: keswickbrewery.co.uk

BEERS: Keswick Gold, Keswick Bitter, Thirst Run, Thirst Quencher

TOURS? Yes, book via the website

TAP ROOM? Yes, The Fox Tap, opened October 2019

STOCKED: Local shops & bars

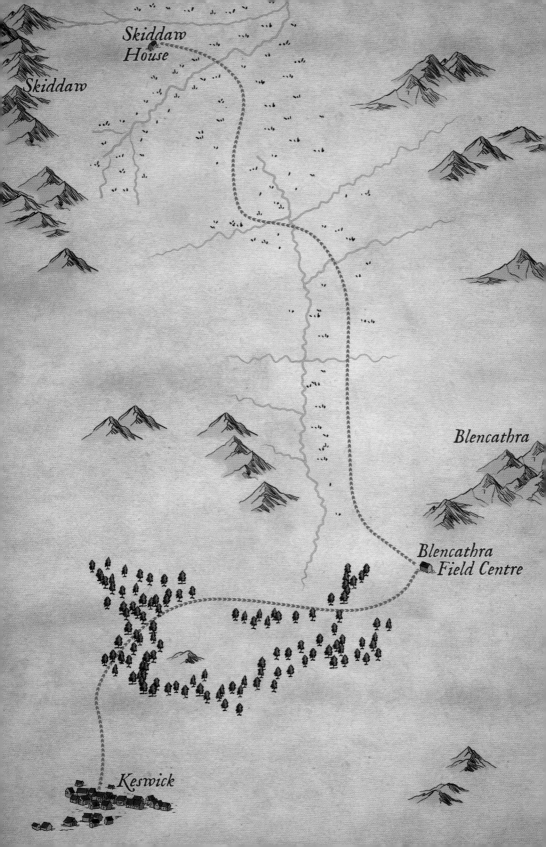

Oohhh matron!

- **Start**: Sunnyside Guesthouse, Keswick
- **End**: Skiddaw House Youth Hostel
- **Distance**: 4.8 miles/ 7.7KM
- **Terrain**: Tarmac, hard track, soft ground
- **Transportation**: Not available

SUNNYSIDE GUESTHOUSE IS UTTERLY FABULOUS and the reason I barely slept a wink had absolutely nothing to do with the room and everything to do with the rapidly expanding clegg bite on my arm. Things were not looking good. I was so drained after the exertions of the previous few days, all I wanted to do was sleep and, here I was, in an enormous comfy bed being driven insane by an insect bite. Even the Piriton failed to knock me out.

I've often thought that bites from animals, and insects, should be in direct proportion to their size. For example a midge, gnat, or clegg bite should be mildly irritating but nothing more. Clearly a bear or crocodile bite should, and would, hurt a lot more. It just seemed vastly unfair that I was suffering so much thanks to a creature roughly the size of my little fingernail.

Over breakfast we chatted to Paul and Nicky. They'd moved up from Derbyshire in June 2018 and Paul, who is a keen walker, describes the Lake District as his 'spiritual home' – something I understood completely. I've never got my head around local snobbery; I really didn't have a lot of say over where I was born and raised, but I knew when I found a place that I belonged. I can't explain quite *why* I feel so at home here, I just know that I do.

They took over Sunnyside Guesthouse in July 2018 and have been busy ever since, and I'm really not surprised; the place is beautifully decorated with lots of thoughtful touches and the bathrooms are stocked with

Sunny smiles at Sunnyside

local products. Being environmentally friendly is a big thing for them too – they recycle just about everything and even do all their own laundry so they can ensure they only use environmentally friendly detergents.

Nicky and Paul were offering a sumptuous breakfast, which Steve took full advantage of.

Thank you tasty porridge!

I felt so rough that all I could manage was a bowl of freshly prepared fruit salad and some yoghurt. I knew I needed more food, but I simply couldn't face it.

Everyone inspected my arm. We decided to nip over to the walk in medical centre just to get it checked as we were about to head into the middle of nowhere for 24 hours but, when we got to the medical centre it was rammed and we would have been there ages. I'll admit I have zero patience and hated the thought of being way behind for the rest of the day so decided to swallow another Piriton, smear on another layer of cream and hope for the best.

Back at Sunnyside Paul offered to walk with us 'just for the first half hour or so' and we were delighted to have him with us. He really is excellent company and an extra pair of hands to pull the cask was more than welcome, seeing as I was pretty much out of action on that front.

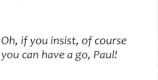

Oh, if you insist, of course you can have a go, Paul!

Such enthusiasm!

I even offered my porterage service, taking pity on Beth and her arm, and gave her a ride on the cask. Only a few yards though, didn't want her getting used to it!

Unfortunately, it wasn't till this moment that I had remembered the idea seeded from Peter at Unsworth's on day two regarding Caskimedes' floating capabilities; re-enacting Dam Busters! There would have been a bit of backtracking to Derwent Water where I thought about hurling it into the lake and watching it bounce. Should it not have bounced I would have blamed it on the fact it was the wrong Derwent …

What a fine host to escort us all this way

We left Keswick heading along the Cumbria Way up to Latrigg car park – a good 45-minute walk. At the top I readied myself to bid farewell to Paul. 'I'll just give it another half hour,' he said, grabbing the trolley and heading off along the track. We chatted happily to people we passed on the way and it wasn't long before we were down in Brundholme looking at the hill up to Blencathra Field Studies Centre, our next rendezvous.

'Well,' I said, turning to Paul. 'Thank you so much for your help.'

He peered up the hill. 'I'll just give it another half hour or so, might as well finish the walk now.' And that was it. Not content with looking after our every need in the guesthouse, he also did sterling work helping Steve transport the cask all the way to the study centre. When we finally reached there we weren't saying goodbye to our landlord, we were saying goodbye to a new friend. That's my favourite part of these crazy adventures, and this is going to sound really cheesy, but I just don't care, we make so many new friends along the way.

Talking of friends ... with Paul now heading back down to Sunnyside, presumably to explain to Nicky why 'just half an hour' had turned into closer to four hours, we sat and munched our lunch as we awaited the arrival of Debs and Andy, two of my favourite friends on account of the fact that they both left 'sane and sensible' behind quite some time ago.

Casky travelling in style

Before long they rocked up, together with Debs' carer, Jane. For those that have never encountered Debs her back story is that she was a keen and active hiker before developing a degenerative spinal condition that has left her in a wheelchair. As she puts it, she's 'fed up of the sad music' which generally accompanies her story and is simply hell bent on getting out there and enjoying life at full pelt.

She is aided and abetted in this mission by husband Andy and her Terrain Hopper, a most magnificent machine which enables her to climb mountains, ford streams and, most importantly at this precise moment in time, help us get a beer cask and two heavy rucksacks up to Skiddaw House Youth Hostel.

We perhaps spent longer than we should have mucking around in the car park trying to figure out the best way to transport everything. The beer cask, at Debs' insistence, was strapped to the back of her Terrain Hopper, making it look like a giant can of NoS which would fire her up the mountain at any moment.

As we walked up to Skiddaw House I pondered the possibilities of adding a can of NoS to Debs' wheelchair. She's got a great sense of adventure; I reckon she'd be up for it.

The question of how to transport her regular wheelchair up there – so she could get around the Youth Hostel – was resolved when we strapped all the rucksacks into it and promised to take it in turns pushing it. Jane, a properly qualified nurse, turned out to be an expert in wheelchair pushing – I was far too wussy with it and took too long navigating the rocks and drops along the way, although when I saw Jane careering along the track I did wonder how her patients had fared when she'd taken them out for a spin ...

Honestly, I fear for my old age having seen how Beth handles a wheelchair and the lessons she was now getting from Jane.

Me and Debs wandered along together, putting the world to rights, while Steve, Andy and Jane brought up the rear with the wheelchair and empty trolley. Debs is a trailblazer when it comes to making the outdoors accessible and was Julia Bradbury's accessibility expert. Julia heads up 'The Outdoor Guide', a website with hundreds of free walks available to download, right across the country and Debs is at the forefront of

We have terrain, and we're hopping all over it.

pioneering accessible routes, plus the local accommodations and pubs, cafes etc. to ensure everything is fully accessible for those requiring additional assistance.

One of the things we chatted about was how the mindset of the self-employed often differed from those in a regular job. Just about all of the self-employed people we knew had a 100 per cent 'let's go for it' attitude. They weren't afraid to try, and took failure in their stride, rather than let it put them off trying something new and/or radical. Lots

of other folks talked a good story but always had an excuse for why they hadn't thrown caution to the wind and just cracked on. Personally I couldn't face the thought of reaching my old age and wondering 'what if?' I find that far more terrifying than failure.

Up at the Youth Hostel there was a fair degree of mucking around as we posed for photos outside before settling down in front of the fire. I love hosting so willingly volunteered to cook dinner and disappeared off to the hostel shop for my supplies. For pudding they

Luckily Andy had the power to haul our weighty collecting tins up the hill

Skiddaw House: bring your crazy adventures here

Look at those mischievous faces...

had a selection of steamed sponges in a variety of flavours which led to an entire evening of Carry On-esque double entendres.

I bobbed my head through the door. 'Right, who wants Spotted Dick?' Everyone dissolved into childish giggles. My enquiries about Sticky Toffee Pudding were met with mild sniggers and when I asked who wanted a 'moist treacle sponge' I genuinely thought we'd need the paramedics.

Sticky Ginger anyone?

The 'kitchen' was a series of hobs around the huge living/ dining area so I could cook and keep up with the ridiculous banter at the same time. The other guests, a father and grown up son from Cockermouth and an American couple, had no option but to descend into our alternative reality and we all shared a thoroughly splendid evening, full of lots of laughter which I still look back on as one of the highlights of the entire trip.

Looking out onto the fells

Hesket Newmarket Brewery, home to our trusty trolley

Our beer of choice for the evening was from Hesket Newmarket Brewery. It's the nearest brewery to the youth hostel and they were the folks who had been kind enough to loan us our trolley. We knew we couldn't reach them on the hike so had nipped in to see them before we set off. Nathan is the head brewer and manager and he filled us in on their unique back story.

The brewery is owned and run by the village as a co-operative, with everyone involved contributing in some way. They produce a distinctive range of traditional beers with a modern twist. When Jim and Liz Fearnley originally started the brewery back in 1988, the world of beer was a lot different, 'craft beer' really wasn't a thing, and it was so hard to get into the regular pubs that they decided to by their own – The Old Crown in the middle of the village.

Did you know that The Old Crown is reputed to be King Charles' favourite pub? He regularly visits when he's in Cumbria and enjoys a nice pint. I wonder if we could get him to help wheel the trolley one day?

The brewery is run by locals

The pub and brewery trundled along together for ten years before Jim retired. Rather than lose this vital part of village life, the locals got together and bought both the pub and the brewery and that's how it continues. Today they produce a range of six 'core beers', their best now probably being 'Haystacks', with two or three others brewed for special occasions. They don't offer brewery tours and they are not profit focused, instead their aim is to keep the brewery secure and ensure employment for the many locals involved in the production process. It was the perfect beer to accompany a comforting night in with friends.

A cosy evening round the table with friends – who could ask for more?

Raring to go

As we drank beer, all sitting around the fire, the evening, descended into a lot of mucking around and micky taking – the sort of micky taking that can only happen amongst good friends.

Debs: 'I'm exhausted, I won't be staying up late.'

Andy: 'Why are you so tired? You've been sat down all bloody day!'

Me and Steve had been stuck together for over a week and, much as we love each other dearly, it was wonderful to properly relax and enjoy the company of Debs, Andy and Jane. Before bedtime I sought out Jane's professional advice about my bite. She looked at it then studied my Piriton packet, asking how many I'd taken.

'Three so far today,' I answered.

'Take two before you go to sleep. If nowt else it'll knock you out.'

With that sound advice ringing in my ears, I made my way upstairs and, spoiler alert, enjoyed the best night's sleep of the entire trek.

It was such a peaceful location. In fact, the only thing disturbing the peace was us. I think I heard Beth blundering around in the night looking for the loo. Or maybe it was bats. Hard to tell.

*****

Update: Of all the updates we've written since we first took off on this adventure, this is by far the hardest to add. Following a short, brutal but brave, battle with cancer in 2021, Andy sadly passed away in July of that year.

Debs organised the most amazing farewell for him, and I shared the story above when I was invited to say a few words. Mine was one of dozens of stories, all told with lots of love, plenty of laughter and more than a few tears.

He really was a truly wonderful person, who touched so many lives in so many positive ways, and I hope that anyone reading this will remember the story above and smile. I know he would have liked that.

*****

BREWERY: Hesket Newmarket Brewery

WEBSITE: hesketbrewery.co.uk

BEERS: Helvellyn Gold, Brim Fell IPA, Haystacks

TOURS? By prior appointment only

TAP ROOM? The Old Crown Pub, Hesket Newmarket

STOCKED: Local shops & bars and Skiddaw House Youth Hostel

Skiddaw House

Skiddaw

Bassenthwaite

Bassenthwaite Lake

Life of a 'Life of a Mountain' bloke

- **Start:** Skiddaw House Youth Hostel
- **End:** Bassenthwaite Village
- **Distance:** 5.6 miles/ 9KM
- **Terrain:** Mostly hardtrack
- **Transportation:** Not available

I HAD THE SORT OF SLEEP that Disney makes films about. An epic, slept for 100 years, world-could-have-ended-and-I-wouldn't-have-noticed sleep. It was awesome. And very much needed. Skiddaw Youth Hostel is the living definition of the 'middle of nowhere' and all that peace and quiet, plus a lot of laughs with good friends (and perhaps not entirely unrelated, several beers, and two Piriton pills), had finally done the trick. I woke up well rested and my arm was finally reducing in size.

Over breakfast we got chatting to Suzy and Martin who run the hostel and I asked them what it was like to live somewhere so remote.

'It's not really remote' came the reply.

I looked out the window at the endless hills, a lone sheep bleated in the distance and the nearest civilisation, down in Keswick, was several miles away, not even in sight. 'How so?'

'Well, it's just the illusion of remote – yes, we are a long way from the town, but it's never quiet here, there are always people around.'

Fair point, there had been nine of us last night; the hostel can take up to twenty, and it's rarely empty. Throughout the summer there are folks booked in, others stopping in to make tea and coffee (available so long as they are open) and, during the winter they often host large groups – stag or hen parties, walking groups etc.

Herdwick gridlock

Truly off-grid

'People book here on purpose,' explained Suzy. 'They want to escape the phones, wifi etc., they know what they're getting and most people see it as an escape.'

This sounds like the sort of thing I would like, although I know that I'd miss my gadgets eventually. But a few days 'off grid' with only sheep to talk to, definitely has an appeal; in fact, I always talk to the sheep when I'm out on the fells.

Suzy and Martin moved into the hostel directly after working in Turkey, so as well as the remoteness they also had to reacclimatise to the cold. They moved in and opened their doors in November 2015; astute readers will recognise that as being one month before Storm Desmond hit, bringing most of Cumbria to a sudden, rain soaked, halt.

Throughout that winter Suzy was commuting down into Keswick every day for her office job, which was needed while they got the business off the ground. There's a ford to cross on the way down the track which they described as being 'exciting' that winter. I think their idea of exciting and mine are probably quite different.

Life can be pretty full on looking after such a remote place, with maintenance, welcoming guests and making sure the place is well stocked (Martin drives down into Cockermouth once a week, then pops over to Workington to sort the laundry out), even 'bins day' is a challenge as their bins are at the end of the track, four miles away, together with the box for their incoming post. They still get plenty of exploring done though and both regularly run, and cycle, around the surrounding fells. ('Why run?' 'Because you can get further.' Oh, ok.)

Our conversation progressed to the sorts of things many of us often think but rarely ask – what about the sewage? They're far too far away to be connected to the mains (their water comes from a nearby beck), and the average sewerage truck wouldn't make it up the track, so where does it all go?

That's my wife, always asking awkward questions. They should let her on Question Time one night, just for a laugh. The politicians wouldn't know what had hit them. The other week she was asking why tea gets weaker when you add milk, but coffee doesn't. Or if a long jump is aligned to the direction of the earth's rotation, does it affect the distance someone can jump. I often wonder what goes on in that mind, but, to be honest, I think it's best not to know.

Turns out that they have a large septic tank which is emptied once a year. This is unpleasant at the best of times, with a tractor pulling a trailer of 'oil drums' up the track to the hostel. Once there the sewage is pumped from the tank, into the drums, and off it trundles back down the hill. All well and good, until one year, in the middle of an incredibly hot summer, the trailer got a puncture just as it left the hostel. There was no option but to leave it there for two whole weeks, in blazing sunshine, while a replacement wheel was sourced and fitted. Nice ...

Suzy and Martin are absolutely lovely and have built a popular, warm, friendly and welcoming business in stunning, if unforgiving, surroundings. We were sorry to be leaving, but our date for the day, Terry Abraham, was due any moment.

To be honest, I was a little awestruck at walking with Terry, especially as we'd need to be taking photos along the way, but he turned out to be a thoroughly nice bloke and we had plenty of laughs as we made our way down the track.

Terry Abraham: cask-lifter extraordinaire

For those who don't know him, Terry is a film maker and the man behind the 'Life of a Mountain' series of films. It began with Scafell Pike, then Blencathra and, when we met with him, he was busy working on 'Helvellyn'. I felt a bit bad about hogging him for most of the day as the sun was shining and conditions for filming were perfect, but they were also perfect for walking so I decided to make the most of it and enjoy the day.

I've been trying to find a way to describe Terry – not physically, you can see that in the photos – but what's he really like? A simple word, or phrase, really won't do it – he's a ball of energy and always seems to be on the go. He is, rightfully so, incredibly proud of the magnificent films he's made (why is it so un-British to be proud of something you've done?) but, at the same time, he's also very humble and down to earth and didn't once try to interfere or offer unwanted advice when I was trying to get suitable photos of him and Steve wandering along the track together.

It was so much fun spending time with someone who is as thoroughly nerdy about the fells as we are. We'd dealt with 'How do you pronounce Scafell Pike' and 'Was there ever really a chapel at Chapel in the Hause' before we even left the hostel. Being used to hauling heavy camera gear up mountains, he laughed when we said our cask was heavy and promptly hoisted it over his head.

I loved his frankness; when, a few days earlier, we'd announced we were going to cancel our hike up Helvellyn due to the heat, everyone had been sympathetic and told us we were doing the right thing. What had Terry thought?

'Get up the bloody mountain!'

Good man. I knew Terry was on my side. Even if he did make me feel like a bit of a wuss when he hoisted Casky and trolley above his head. Said it weighted the same as his filming gear. Bet he's never swum with his filming gear.

In a world awash with political game playing, Terry's straight talking was an absolute breath of fresh air. We chatted about how he made his films, and the mind numbing amount of dedication and preparation that does into them. Honestly, for every minute seen on the screen there is at least a day, usually more, of hard work behind it. He also talked about the importance of being on the same wavelength as Freddy, the composer who scores all the incredible music for Terry's films.

'I have skill, but that man has got real talent,' as Terry put it.

We paused for coffee and cake half way down. Terry lit up a hand rolled fag and we all sat on the floor, in the sunshine, putting the world to rights. His grandmother survived the concentration camps of World War II and clearly had a strong influence on Terry.

'She told me to always tell the truth, even if people don't like it,' he said, which perhaps explains his refreshing openness.

Putting the world to rights along the route to Bassenthwaite

Casky posing by a waterfall

Each day, when we walked with someone we barely knew, I worried about what we talk about. Would it be polite conversation? Would there be any of those awkward silences? Would we end up discussing the weather for five hours or more? But there was none of that, everyone we walked with was superb company, with so many interesting stories to tell, and Terry was absolutely no exception, and I was quite sad when we waved him off at our parting point.

Me and Steve continued on down towards Bassenthwaite village. We got a bit lost along the way and stopped another couple to check our directions. We managed to stand in the middle of a field with them and have a full five-minute conversation, without anyone once referencing the beer cask and large trolley stood between us. British reserve at its very finest.

We made it to our hotel. Easily the poshest place of the entire trip. Well, I say 'posh', perhaps 'expensive' would be a better word, but there was nowhere else available in the village. We were clearly their stinkiest guests and I don't think we made a good first impression as we rolled our cask across their marble floor in a cloud of dust with the smell of a long stinky hike swirling around us. As we checked in they asked if we wanted to book breakfast for £14.95 each. I looked mildly horrified.

It's definitely this direction...

'It's cheaper to book it now,' they reassured us. 'If you pay in the morning, it's £16 each.'

£16? For breakfast? No chance. I know I'm tight and our budget is small, but £16 for breakfast? No flipping chance! I thought back to the wonderful porridge at Sunnyside Guesthouse and wondered if we could persuade them to deliver?

We hauled the cask to our room, up and around many flights of stairs, the sound of hollow metal clanking echoed the marbled corridors. We quickly freshened up, then raced down to Lake District Wildlife Park where we thought we'd arranged for a nice quiet tootle around and a meeting with one of the keepers.

'Where's your cask?' asked Lucy, Education and Marketing Officer and thoroughly lovely lady.

'Erm, back in our room,' I said. 'I thought we were having a night off.'

'Nope – we've arranged for you to go in with the Tapirs, we thought it might be fun.'

I'll be honest; I couldn't have picked a Tapir out of a line-up at that stage. 'Which ones are the Tapirs?' I asked, lamely.

'You'll love them!' she beamed, as we followed her back out into the sunshine. 'They're like great big Labradors.' I'd met Lucy when we'd both attended a two day Outdoor First Aid course earlier in the year.

We arrived at the Tapir enclosure. To my uneducated eye they looked like a cross between an anteater and a boar, but they seemed friendly enough. One of them stuck his nose on the electric fence and jumped back in shock. The electric fence wasn't new; he just hadn't quite figured it out yet.

Not wanting to miss out on any potentially new experience we jumped in their van and shot off to pick up the cask. I was about to spend time inside an enclosure with wild animals. I was beyond excited! This isn't a gimmick, the wildlife park is focused on education and conservation and up close experiences with some of the animals is just one part of helping people get to know, and understand, wildlife a little better.

Our safety briefing complete, me, Steve, and our trusty cask entered the enclosure under the watchful eye of Lucy and Vicky, the head keeper. As we sat on the floor the Tapirs snuffled around, they were very inquisitive and, thankfully, friendly, but were refusing to pose for photographs. We

Hello, handsome!

tried putting food on the top of the cask to keep their attention in the right place – they may be like a Labrador in temperament, but at around 200KG each, we couldn't haul them into the perfect position, so we chatted in the sunshine while we awaited the perfect pose.

With Lucy's 'Labradors'

Tapirs are known to have an unpredictable temperament but I wasn't about to pass up the chance to get up close to them. Lucy seemed to know what she was doing. I was also a bit peckish and their food didn't look all bad. For a moment I pondered stealing a sunflower seed, but one of them eyed me suspiciously, as if reading my mind. I withdrew my hand and tied to look innocent.

'What could we, as ordinary folks, do to protect wild animals like this?' I asked.

'Don't breed!' was the swift reply. It was said jokingly but wasn't as harsh as it first seems. The more people who live on the planet, the more we have to consume to stay alive, and it's inevitable that we will encroach more and more onto the environment of other creatures. It's basic maths. And physics. And biology.

The other things they suggested were being mindful of where our things come from – food, clothing etc. Palm oil and cotton, for example, can have a hugely negative impact on the natural world, with habitats being destroyed to fuel our need. And then there's the obvious advice of recycling, not buying new and reusing things wherever we can to reduce our consumption.

During our chat Muffin and Xeno (the tapirs) had managed to pose a little, and we'd managed to learn a lot. Some of the food we'd sprinkled on the top of 'Tapbier' the cask for them got caught around the edges and stayed there for the rest of the hike. Whenever I saw it, it always made me think of them and smile.

Back at the hotel we enjoyed a quick dip in the pool before wolfing down an adequate but very expensive dinner (I was far too tired to argue about my sweet chilli and chickpea burger being barely warm), before climbing into our very expensive bed and wondering what we'd eat for breakfast. One thing was certain; whatever it was would not be costing us £16 each!

Flies. There were flies everywhere. I've never been in a restaurant with so many flies. We got through half the meal then moved to a table recently vacated by someone else. It was only marginally better. And they had no local beers on tap. Ironic that the most expensive place we were staying in was only marginally better than the cheapest. At least there were no 'crumbs' on my bed here, and I didn't have to strip it in the morning.

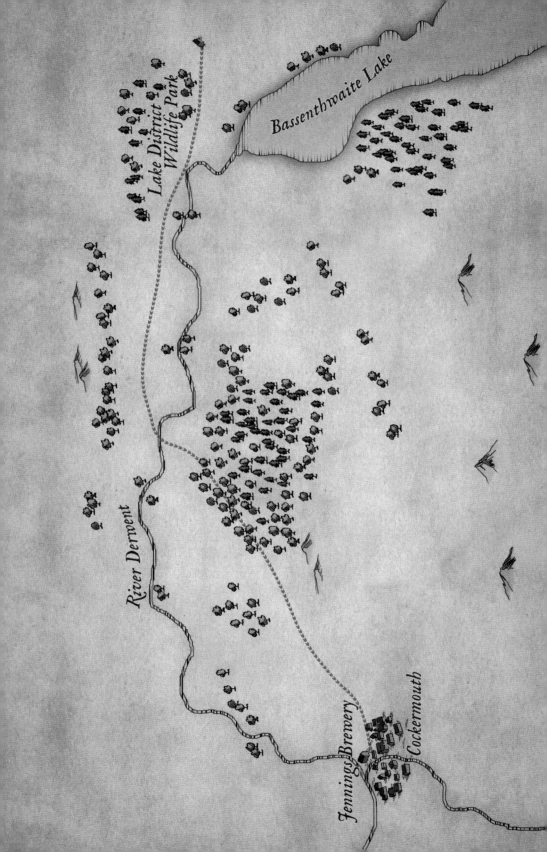

Bassenthwaite Lake

Lake District Wildlife Park

River Derwent

Jennings Brewery

Cockermouth

Rescue me

 Start: Bassenthwaite village

 End: Jennings Bewery

Distance: 7 miles/ 11.2KM

Terrain: Hard track and tarmac

Transportation: Bus X4 Gold

TODAY I WAS NOT WORRIED about transporting the cask, but I was worried about breakfast – although not worried enough to pay £16 each for it. We ransacked the free tea and coffee in the room (the biscuits had mysteriously vanished the moment we arrived) and pondered the day as we crunched a couple of Belvitas. Then I had a brainwave – the zoo had an excellent cafe and I was sure I remembered them advertising breakfast; we had to walk right past their front door and it would be rude not to pop in and support a local business.

The only downside was that they didn't open until 10am, so we just needed to kill time until then. The problem with that was that we were spending the day with ex-Gurkha and Mountain Rescue volunteer Stephen Crowsley. I was pretty sure that, given his background, Stephen would be bang on time and would arrive well fed and watered for the day ahead. I was right. Stephen was also the reason that I wasn't worried about transporting the cask for the day; Terry Abraham may have hoisted it above his head for a photo but I was pretty sure Stephen would be able to dribble it like a basketball and slam dunk it into the mash tub at Jennings Brewery (our finish point) if the mood took him.

Not only was he an ex-Gurkha but he was pretty good at being a Sherpa, taking the cask for most of the journey, making my day a lot lighter.

I was impressed, and a little bit intimidated, from the moment we met Stephen. He was utterly lovely, incredibly well spoken (something you'd expect from an ex-equerry to Prince Philip) and had impeccable manners. The intimidation part was all down to me – here I was with someone who could survive the jungle and withstand horrendous conditions without batting an eyelid – what would he make of me? Would he think I was too out of shape to continue a hike like this? Would he be appalled that we hadn't had breakfast and needed to stop at the zoo? Would he judge our backpacks harshly and think we were carrying too much? Or not enough? It's amazing how we torture ourselves, isn't it? Turns out I had nothing whatsoever to worry about – Stephen was so thoroughly lovely that, even if he had thought any of those things, he would never in a million years say anything. (Oh my god, what if he did think them?!)

We explained our breakfast situation to him and set off in the sunshine towards the zoo, dealing with the pleasantries along the way. We had to hang around for ten minutes for the cafe to open and I left Stephen and Steve outside chatting while I went to get a couple of Cumberland sausage buns. I was focused on my mission and not about to get distracted by anything.

Returning outside, clutching two sausage buns and a three-foot clip on lemur tail, I had a bit of explaining to do.

Our route was simple – follow the lonning along past the zoo, then up and over Watch Hill and down into Cockermouth – so we could concentrate on talking (and eating the divine sausage buns) rather than navigating.

Stephen was utterly fascinating company; following twelve years in the armed forces, during which time he served in the Falklands and spent lots of time in the jungle (he had a number of stories involving leeches which made my rogue insect bite pale into insignificance), he moved to the USA before returning back to Blighty and settling in Cumbria.

I was keen to find out more about Mountain Rescue – we were raising funds for them as we went, and will be donating a portion of the profits of this book to them too, but what does it take to be a Mountain Rescue volunteer? In my mind you needed to be fit as a flea, know the fells like the back of your hand and probably have some sort of climbing and medical background. Turns out I was only partly right.

As Stephen explained you don't necessarily have to be fast, but you

Stephen Crowsley, an officer and a gentleman

do need to be fit enough to carry a load across rough terrain; a long rescue may take more than a few hours so rescuers need to ideally arrive in waves. The first guys on the scene are generally the most medically qualified, with credentials very similar to paramedics. They can assess and / or begin treatment while other rescuers arrive. If you've ever been on a first aid training course you'll have an idea how exhausting giving CPR can be, especially over an extended period, so having people to swap in and out with is essential. On one rescue Stephen described how a genuine mistake by two climbers led to a nine-hour rescue involving twenty two Mountain Rescue volunteers.

For potential rescuers there's a weekend 'test' which involves map reading and navigation assessment, as well as the ability to move comfortably at night on steep ground on the fells, and then usually a probationary period for everyone involved to suss out suitability. But Mountain Rescue isn't just about racing around the fells; there are a lot of backroom folks needed too, including people to do the accounts, managing publicity etc. Most of the call outs don't attract media attention so no-one does it for the glory. In fact it takes a very particular kind of person to put their own life at risk, at a moment's notice, on a dark, wet, rainy, Saturday night, in the middle of dinner, and go out onto

On the way to Cockermouth

the fells to rescue a complete stranger, and, not only not get paid for it, but get very little recognition either. Hats off to the lot of them I say.

I'm always impressed that Mountain Rescue never judge, even if someone has done something the rest of us would question, MR just go up and get the job done, they never want anyone to feel afraid to call them, whatever the situation. Like Beth says, I don't know how they do it.

Home of contented cows and satisfied sheep

Sausage and egg you say, with chilli sauce?

As we wandered through a farm a drone buzzed high over our heads. There, standing in the shade of the barn was the owner of the drone. I had an idea. I wandered over to say 'hello' and explain what we were up to.

'Could you take our photo?' I asked. Cheeky, I know, but as my sister-in-law puts it, 'shy bairns get nowt'.

'Of course,' he laughed. Like everyone else we encountered, he clearly thought we were nuts. He manoeuvred the drone into position as we all smiled skywards. I gave him my card so he could email them to us and, looking at them now, they put me in mind of the album cover for *Band on the Run*. I definitely think we look a little shady and can envisage the photo beneath a banner headline on the front of the local paper: 'Three ne'er-do-wells kidnap beer cask; last spotted near Cockermouth, the general public are advised not to approach them.'

Stephen delighted us with so many stories as we continued on towards Cockermouth – some touching, like the time a very elderly ex-Gurkha in Nepal recognised his uniform and insisted on honouring him by cooking the only egg their chicken had laid that day. Despite Stephen's protests the gentleman's wife prepared the egg with great care before presenting it to their honoured guest. In return Stephen took a photograph of them on an instamatic camera he had and gave them the picture. They lived in an incredibly poor village and although they had been married for over 50 years, this was the only photograph they had ever had taken of them together.

Jennings Brewery

I liked the story about the time a combination of poor light and fatigue caused him and his colleagues to mistake a flock of marching penguins for an invading army. That's an easy mistake to make; have you seen sheep's eyes when they catch a beam of headtouch light at night? They look like something from Scooby Doo and can give you quite a fright on a late walk.

I did take the opportunity to ask what a man with survival expertise and a serving member of Penrith Mountain Rescue Team (part of Lake District Search and Mountain Rescue) considers to be the perfect sandwich for a long hike.

'Sausage and egg, with sweet chilli sauce, on toasted bread, so it doesn't go soggy.' Great tip!

Our destination was Jennings Brewery, on the banks of the river. Most of the breweries we visited for this book were more modern and much smaller than Jennings – this was certainly the largest place we would be calling in to. The brewery was founded in Lorton (just down the road) in 1828, and in 1881 it moved to Cockermouth in, what was at the time, state of the art facilities. Today it is a glorious collection of old red brick and white painted buildings and their iconic chimney is part of the skyline of the town.

We arrived under the famous archway, just in time for a quick pint of Sneck Lifter before our guided tour. We hadn't demanded to have the tour to ourselves, it just turned out that way. I immediately had a question.

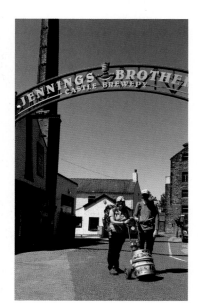

'What's a Sneck Lifter?' I'd not grown up in Cumbria and was curious to find out.

Apparently 'sneck' is a Cumbrian expression for a latch on the door and the phrase 'sneck lifter' refers to having enough money to go down the pub for a pint.

Perfect weather for a brewery tour!

IRENE COURT
(TEETOTAL LANE)

Let's not go there...

The brewery tour was fascinating and informative. By now we were very familiar with the brewing process but every single brewery has its own quirks, and Jennings was no exception. The timbers in the building have been dated back to old ships' timbers from the eighteenth century, they have their own well from which they draw all the water for their beers and, although they have a lot of state of the art machinery, they also have a lot of the original wooden fixtures and fittings.

Apparently giant beer vats made entirely of wood were phased out in the early nineteenth century following a beer flood in London (nothing to do with Jennings!). A vat exploded and around 300,000 gallons of beer flooded a nearby slum, killing eight people. The event would have bankrupted the brewery but it was saved when HMRC issued a rebate on duty for the beer lost. Although many of the vats at Jennings, and elsewhere, look wooden from the outside, they have stainless steel interior cladding.

Impressive machinery on the Jennings tour

A picture gallery of some of the forbears of the Brewery

Obviously they take their brewing very seriously and store a culture of their yeast in a 'yeast store' down in London. It might sound extreme but it was a godsend in 2009 and 2015 when the brewery was flooded. They brought back just one teaspoon of the yeast from London and built up the brews until they were back to capacity again.

Jeremy Pettman, the head brewer, and Jacqui Cown, our guide have many decades of experience between them so my advice if you go there on a tour is to ask lots of questions as they are both an absolute mine of fascinating information.

Following the tour we stayed to sample a few beers in the bar and wandered out on their patio overlooking the river. We were drinking a fair amount of beer, but a lot less than our ancestors for whom beer would have been much more common. Before the cleanliness of water could be guaranteed, beer was generally safer to drink and was even given to young children. Even the word 'toddler' comes from kids toddling around after drinking beer. Imagine what social services would make of that today?

We sadly bid farewell to Stephen in the sunshine of Cockermouth high street and headed for our accommodation to refresh and revive ourselves. I was giving a talk at The New Bookshop in the evening, and I needed to go back over my notes.

Jennings Brewery, situated where the River Cocker meets the River Derwent

As a writer I spend a lot of time at my desk, at home, often in my pyjamas, bashing away on the laptop. Obviously I know that people will read what I write, but I'm still taken aback when people willingly give up their evening and pay good money to come and hear me talk. Frankly there are many times when Steve would gladly pay me to shut up!

My topic for the evening was our *Gin, Cake and Rucksacks* book, which had also involved a visit to Cockermouth, and an update on our journey thus far with the cask. The New Bookshop is an absolute gem of a place and is the sort of bookshop every town should have. Catherine, the owner, is fabulous and has a stream of authors coming in to give talks throughout the year. There's a cafe there too so the refreshments were superb with plenty of cake to soak up the gin samples on offer.

A crowd of 35 people turned up to listen to me, which blew me away. Many of them bought our books afterwards and chatted with us as we signed them. There were a few familiar faces in the crowd too, which was lovely. The person I was most surprised to see was Jeanette, who'd hauled the cask with us up and over Helvellyn, I honestly thought she'd be sick to death of us after what we made her do.

All done and dusted we headed off to our very first night in an Airbnb – more of that tomorrow.

'What's on the list for tomorrow?' asked Steve.

'Well, first up we're off to Wordsworth House, then we're walking twelve miles to Workington, and stopping at Tractor Shed brewery on the way.'

'You don't do "rest days" do you?'

'Not really ... but the day after that will be a bit easier, I promise.'

'Yeah, right.'

He knows me so well.

BREWERY: Jennings Brewery

BEERS: Sneck Lifter, Cumberland, Atomic Theory IPA

TOURS? No

TAP ROOM? No

STOCKED: Extensively across the county in bars and shops, but no longer brewed in Cumbria

*****

Update: Covid hit the Jennings brewery hard. In May 2020 Marston's (who owned Jennings) merged with Carlsberg UK. Following the pandemic, brewery tours never restarted and, in September 2022 local fears were realised when Carlsberg Marston's Brewing Company announced that they were closing this iconic brewery, with all Jennings beers now produced in Burton. At the time of writing the building is on the market. This is a crying shame. As we saw in Ulverston, and will see in Whitehaven, there is a history of large breweries buying and then closing down, successful small breweries. If there's one thing this book has taught us, it's that there is a large, and thirsty, market for small, locally produced, beers.

*****

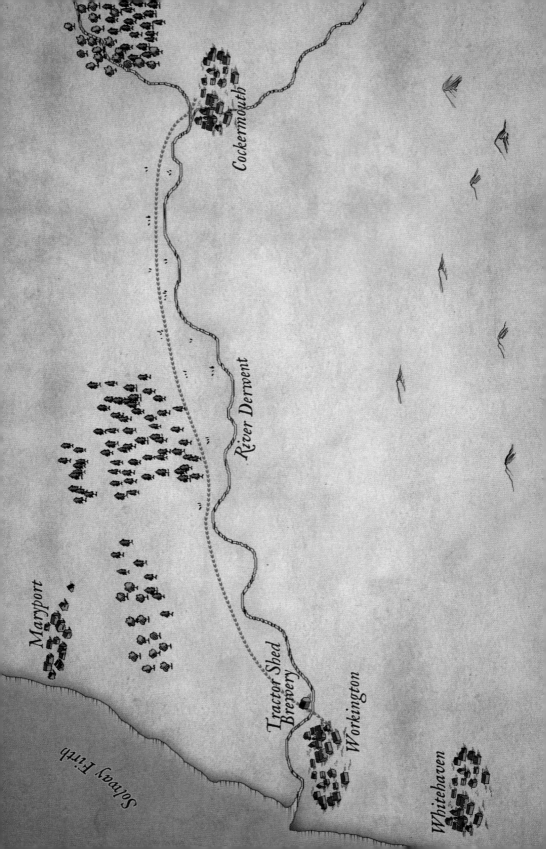

Cockermouth

River Derwent

Maryport

Tractor Shed Brewery

Workington

Whitehaven

Solway Firth

I wandered lonely as a beer cask

- **Start:** Cockermouth
- **End:** Workington
- **Distance:** 8.8 miles/ 14.1KM
- **Terrain:** Mostly tarmac
- **Transportation:** Bus – X6 Gold

OUR FIRST PROPER AIRBNB experience was definitely a good one. Our host, Claire, was pleasant and chatty, but not intrusive and our room was small with lovely views over Cockermouth. As usual, I'd woken up before Steve and, while he grabbed a few more precious minutes of sleep, I lay pondering the whole concept of rest days. I'd never really thought about them but now, here we were, at the start of day twelve with six more days to go, and I was beginning to see how they could be useful. The next time I plan a ridiculous adventure, I'll be sure to include some.

Our first stop of the day was at Wordsworth House and Garden at the top of Main Street. I've always thought I should learn more about Wordsworth but, to be brutally honest, I've tried reading his poems and they don't really do it for me, but I was certainly interested in learning more about the man. As it turned out, I learned a lot more about Dorothy than I did about William.

What we learned about William, and Dorothy, Wordsworth

In a nutshell, they were both born in the house, around eighteen months apart. Although there were five children Dorothy and William were always very close and behaved more like twins than brother and sister. Their parents were unconventional for the era and encouraged their children to spend plenty of time outdoors, swimming in the river running along the bottom of the garden and scrambling all over the castle.

For Dorothy, this idyllic childhood came to an abrupt end at the age of six, when her mother died. Dorothy was sent away to live with a cousin of her mother's in Halifax, who was good and kind and taught her how to run a

The beautiful gardens at Wordsworth House

household (an essential skill for Georgian women). The problem was she was separated from William and didn't see him for another nine years. This separation scarred her for life and perhaps explains why they were so close and shared a house in their later years.

As adults they were very much a team when it came to William's writing, with Dorothy being the person who brought order to his creative chaos. She meticulously kept a journal and they would often sit and read it together – it was this precise activity which led to the writing of his famous 'Daffodils' poem. She would then read, and critique, his work before it was published; each poem was the product of close teamwork.

The National Trust team at Wordsworth House go out of their way to devise ways to engage people in the story of the Wordsworths; they host weddings, run endless children's events where the kids get to dress up, try sleeping top to toe in the beds and even get to work in the kitchen. The brilliant news for us was that they were quite happy to encourage adults to dress up too, so off me and Steve went to swap Goretex for Georgian.

I thought Steve looked really rather dapper in his waistcoat and tri-corn hat, but I really wasn't warming to my heavy maid's outfit. Or rather I was warming to it in one way – those outfits are incredibly hot

Beth and Steve as Georgian cask-carriers. Pass me tankard!

and I have no idea how they coped wearing them all day while running up and down the stairs catering to the every whim of the family.

We just did a few hundred yards taking photos and video in front of the house and I was absolutely baking hot and itching to get back into my nice cool t-shirt. It was also the first time I'd been in a skirt for around twelve months; sometimes I almost forget I'm a girl.

Yes I looked quite good in me waistcoat and tri-corn hat, though I thought my brightly multi-coloured Aku walking shoes really brought the 'colonial knee britches and white leg sock look' together. To finish it off I had my pewter tankard of ale while Beth, the fetching maid, pulled 'Wordswort' the cask behind.

Before we headed off towards Workington, our lovely guide ran through some fabulous facts about Georgian food and drink and Wordsworth House. They were so good that I wanted to add them all right here.

- In the 1930s the local council threatened to demolish the house to build a bus station. Thankfully the folks of Cockermouth were having none of it and raised the £1625 needed to buy it and give it to the National Trust, which has opened it to the public since 1939. Phew!
- In 1740 gin was cheaper than food – you could get drunk for a penny and dead drunk for two.
- In 1757, 9000 small children died (that's not a typo!) after being given gin to keep them quiet. It was generally given to them on a piece of rag to suck.
- Alcohol was regularly used in food to preserve it and also to mask the taste of rotting ingredients.
- Cookbooks of the period would usually have several pages on how to disguise the taste of rancid meat.
- Beer assessors would travel around the taverns checking to see if landlords were watering down their beer. They'd do this by wearing leather trousers, pouring some beer on the bench, then sitting in it to see if they stuck to it. If they did, it meant it was the good stuff!
- Local MP James 'Wicked Jimmy' Lowther was very corrupt and once owned the house. He sat in the House of Commons for 27 years, mainly because he would ensure there was free beer on the bar in all of the local taverns for two weeks before the elections.

She also showed us a recipe for 'Capon Ale', but it was revolting. I think I'll let Steve tell you all about that one!

Have your game-keeper get one of your many kitchen servants two large Cocks or Capons (a cockerel that he has castrated) and pluck them (I've added this bit but I assume one wouldn't like feathers in one's brew).

Stoke your cast iron kitchen range and parboil them on the open fire for an hour or more till all the blood is gone.

Make a decoration from the peel of an orange or citron and a little mace.

Cut off the shanks of the capons and throw them away (or the servants may have them as a luxury meal)

Some splendid cooking tips may be gleaned from this esteemed publication

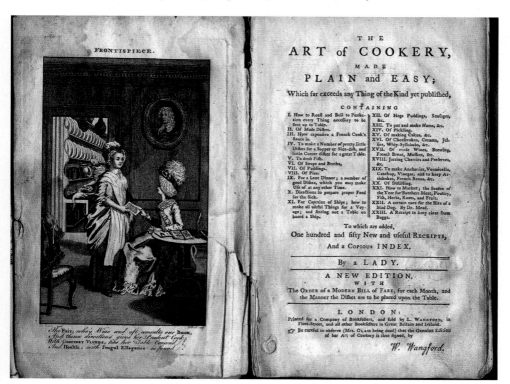

With a chopping knife, mince them bone and all as small as ordinary minced meat.

Put them into a large linen Boulter (sieve bag) then take a Kilderkin (cask 16–18 gallons) sweet and well-seasoned put into it 4 or 5 gallons of strong ale of the first running, new as it is, make in the Kilderkin a large bung-hole and thrust into it the Boulter in which the capons are.

Let them steep in it three days and nights leaving the bung-hole open to work. Then take out the capons, close the bung-hole and let it stand a day and a half after which bottle it off. You may drink it after three days bottling, but it will keep six weeks if closed stopped.

Mmm ... a robust Victorian ale. Don't waste the contents of that Boulter, it would make another hearty broth/stew!

Taken from the 1747 book, 'The Art of Cookery', written 'By a LADY'. The author's name, Hannah Glasse, wasn't used initially as, presumably, it wasn't 'done' to be seen cooking one's own meals, or to be brewing beer!

Anyway, it turns out it was a best seller for a century and, in 1758, she finally added her name as the author, becoming the most famous cookbook author of her time.

She had a couple of other brewing tips too:

'The Best thing for rope bier: Mix two handfuls of bean flour, and one handful of salt, throw this into a kilderkin of beer, don't stop it close till it has done fomenting, then let it stand a month, and draw it off; but sometimes nothing will do with it.'

'When a Barrel of Beer is turned four: To a kilderkin of beer throw in at the bung a quart of oatmeal, lay the bung on loose two or three days, then stop it down close, and let it stand a month. Some throw in a piece of chalk as big as a turkey's egg, and when it has done working stop it close for a month, then tap it.'

It was time for us to take our leave and head west to Workington and the lovely Tractor Shed brewery. Much of the route was along roads. Ok, all of the route was along roads, but they were very lovely roads and, for the most part, very quiet.

When you're doing a walk like this with someone you know so well, what on earth do you talk about? Well, on that particular stretch we discussed a lot of conspiracy theories about the colossal plantation we were walking past. I really can't explain it but there was something very odd about it. Steve has a great tendency to launch into conspiracy theories but, on this occasion, I think he may have been on to something.

Broughton Moor. It looks intriguing on the map and as you walk past you can see old bunkers and green corrugated iron quonset huts. It looks like an old military site, eerily abandoned from the Cold War era, like somewhere I shouldn't be taking photos of or speaking of in public.

After the hike I looked it up, apparently it's a former Royal Naval Armaments Depot. As it's been out of public access for over 50 years it now an ecological haven for a wide variety of plants and animals.

In Seaton we discovered a life-sized model of John Wesley, who preached there in 1752. Obviously we had to pose him with our beer cask, much to the obvious disgust of an elderly lady driving by. Ooops. I checked in with my brother Paul who, in August 2019 became the Methodist Minister for the area and asked if John would have seen the funny side.

To Great Broughton and beyond!

John Wesley, a giant of his time

'No – he wasn't renowned for his sense of humour – but he did enjoy a beer!'

I reckoned we were ok then.

We arrived into Tractor Shed brewery pretty much gasping for a pint and they didn't disappoint.

'Would you like a Hefeweizen?'

'A what?'

'Hefeweizen – here, try one!'

For those, like us, that can't tell a Hefeweizen from a Hasselhoff, the former is a Bavarian wheat beer which gets its unusual taste from the fact that it is fermented at a higher temperature and still has yeast in it. This means it absolutely has to be served cold, or else the yeast would just keep right on fermenting. The latter is less tasteful but is great to sing along to after a few wheat beers.

As always I immediately began asking nosey questions about their background. Graeme started the brewery in 2009 but back then it was called Mitchell Krause using a combination of Graeme's parents' surnames. Graeme had spent many years working for Whitbread down in the southeast, but was unsettled and wanted something new. He tried changing breweries to Carlsberg and then tried his hand as a drinks consultant at a major marketing firm, but none of them did it for him. He was fed up of his long days, his long commutes and never seeing his two young kids – a change was needed!

He'd grown up on the family farm in Workington and his wife Rachel's parents lived in Caldbeck so, in 2009 they returned to their roots and decided to start a beer business. You may recall that 2009 was the year of the 'big crash' when the economy tanked and banks weren't lending money to new start-ups, so they scraped together everything they had and launched in, with no loans or other financial support.

After a few years having their beers brewed by other breweries, they finally opened their own in the family farm's old Tractor Shed in 2013. Graeme openly admits it was a steep learning curve. Rather than attempting to recreate traditional English ales, Graeme and his team (Matt, Alan and Sue) focus their attention on brewing a range of unusual continental beers, packed with flavour and fun. Sales were going well but a spot of market research showed that many people had no idea that they were a local brewer so, they changed their name to Tractor Shed Brewing, got themselves a snazzy new logo and relaunched.

Their beers and their labels are all local and fabulously quirky. Their beers include Jinny Howelt – an old Cumbrian name for an owl, and the label includes a Viking owl. 'Whistling Pig' came about because, like most Cumbrian brewers, they send their old mash grain to a local pig farm. One of the old pigs got very excited every time the mash was delivered but she had a problem with her snout which meant she whistled rather than grunted, so they named a beer after her.

I loved their labels, definitely the best labels we'd seen so far. So much detail on them. Does anyone even look at beer labels properly? Probably not. We spent ages selecting just the right one to stick onto Wordswort. I decided to play closer attention to beer labels in future.

Fabulous labelling from Tractor Shed

Cheers!

The brewery is incredibly relaxed and laid back. They take bookings for tours and events, or you could just drop by on the off chance and see what's going on. They may not have the beer on the pumps but they will have bottles you could buy and, so long as someone is there, there will definitely be someone interesting to chat to. For now, they are a strictly local brewery but are constantly experimenting with new and exciting flavours and, over the coming months, plan to start selling online and maybe expanding beyond the county boundaries. Watch this space!

Like Ulverston at the start of the hike, Workington is another town where their original, and wonderful, old brewery closed. The original

A spick and span tractor shed if ever there was one

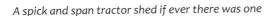

Workington Brewery was founded in 1795 and traded all the way through until 1988. In its later years it went through several changes of ownership before Scottish and Newcastle Breweries finally pulled the plug. Many of the distinctive buildings remain but are now apartment blocks.

We pondered the boom of small brewers as we made our way to the B&B, and how beer is seemingly bucking the trend of globalisation. There is very clearly a market for the vast array of new and exciting beers being produced, and their fan base clearly values small and unique over large and 'consistent' (boring). I sincerely hope they don't get bought out by the 'big guys' and end up like Workington Brewery and Hartley's Brewery in Ulverston.

I'd never really wandered through Workington before and was surprised at how big it was. It couldn't be that far to the B&B, could it? We twisted and turned through the back streets. I was glad we'd decided to cover up our collecting pots with a coat. It just seemed the sensible thing to do in a town – we reckoned there must be a good few hundred quid in those pots by now. We were very grateful whenever anyone made a donation, but I was especially grateful for nice, light, paper donations.

The B&B was just across the road from a Chinese takeaway which we decided to visit for tea – not something we usually do, but it was close and we were knackered and starving. They had cameras in the kitchens so you could see everything being cooked which made the waiting time pass a bit quicker. The food was ok but too salty for me, we don't eat out very often and, when we do, we both find things a bit over-seasoned. Or maybe we're just getting old and grouchy.

BREWERY: Tractor Shed Brewery

WEBSITE: tractor-shed.co.uk

BEERS: Jinny Howlet, Hiefer, Clocker Stout, Whistling Pig, Mowdy Pale Ale

TOURS? Best to check first

TAP ROOM? Yes – open most of the time

STOCKED: Local shops & bars

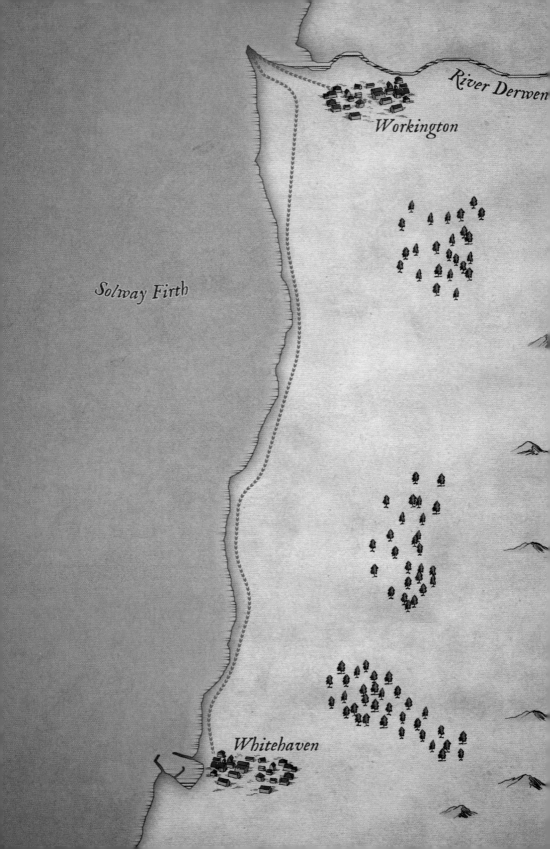

River Derwen

Workington

Solway Firth

Whitehaven

Sister act

 Start: Workington

 End: Gin & Beer It, Whitehaven

Distance: 8.7 miles/ 14KM

Terrain: Tarmac, Hard Track

Transportation: Train – stations at Workington and Whitehaven

I WAS PARTICULARLY EXCITED about today; today we were walking with my big sister Ruth and her husband Ken. Oh, and Mya, their lunatic rescue dog.

Sleep hadn't been brilliant – the B&B was lovely and run by a very nice young couple who had included lots of thoughtful touches, like real milk in a cooler outside our door in the morning instead of those nasty milk pots you usually get. The main downside for us was that it was on quite a busy road and very near a pedestrian crossing. The weather hadn't really cooled down much so we either sweltered with the window shut or lay awake listening to the noise with it open. The upshot was we were starting out exhausted and bleary eyed again.

I always like pedestrian crossings. Until now. The incessant 'beep, beep, beep' at regular intervals throughout the night drove me to distraction. I was glad I'd brought my eye mask with me. Not glamorous, but essential at this time of year in Cumbria when it gets lights at 4am. It wasn't daylight it was keeping out this time though, it was the red, flashing amber, and green of the crossing. The B&B really was as lovely as Beth says, it was just the traffic that was the problem.

We wandered down to the station to meet Ruth and Ken who had travelled all the way up from Kidderminster to join us for the day. We're not the sort of family who live in each other's pockets but we're always there for each other and I was very much looking forward to today's walk.

Ruth is ten years older than I am and Ken is nine years older than her, and both of them are very fit and active and spend a lot of time outdoors walking the dog in the hills around there home or heading off on exciting adventures to the Scottish islands. Neither of them has explored much of Cumbria, although they did spend their honeymoon here and recall a particularly interesting trip to Silloth, not too far up around the coast from where we were.

We passed a plaque for Mary Queen of Scots, claiming she landed here at 7pm on Sunday, May 16th, 1568. How do they know it was 7pm? Did they even have clocks then? And who wrote it down? I'm very suspicious of that plaque.

Our route should have been very straightforward, and it was at first; keep walking west till you meet the sea, then turn left and keep going south. Easy eh? We somehow managed to lose the Cumbria Coastal Way and found ourselves wandering around an industrial estate. We'd navigated for miles across the tops of rugged fells but couldn't find our way off a trading estate, typical. Our navigational skills were not filling Ruth and Ken with confidence …

Don't blame me, I was busy fending off Mya. She's a very friendly dog, but a bit of a lunatic. Beth had put me in charge of navigation while she

A plaque with very particular attention to detail

chatted to Ruth, but I got distracted chatting to Ken. I was expecting (hoping) there would be public access to the shore through the estate but sometimes I find town maps don't have enough detail close up. I can navigate just using sheep trails but hopeless at road names.

Eventually we relocated our path which had been hiding in some bushes all along. It's not the prettiest of paths until you're south of Workington, but keep your eyes on the sea and you'll be fine.

I'd always thought of me and Ruth as being like chalk and cheese, and we are very different in many ways. She has always been more girly than me, although, to be fair, that's really not hard. Anyone who wears a skirt more than once a year is more girly than me. By that token Eddie Izzard is more

With Ruth at the start of the Coast to Coast walk in Workington

girly than me. Not that my sister is anything like Eddie Izzard. I think I'd better stop there before I dig myself in any deeper!

Despite our differences it turns out that we have an awful lot in common. As a kid Ruth remembers playing in a park at the end of their garden, usually with my big brother Paul in tow (they are only eighteen months apart in age whereas I popped along many years later!).

'There was a big tree there, well, I remember it as big, it was probably no more than an over grown bush,' she said. 'I'd often disappear off up to the top branch and sit there for hours watching the birds and looking at everyone else going by down below.'

I'd never climbed that particular tree, but can definitely relate to the idea of escaping into a secret spot. We were in a different house when I was a kid with a long strip of rough ground behind the house. The trees weren't really climbable but I do remember hiding in dens that we'd made in the May bushes.

Although we were both urban kids, with council parks as our only green spaces, we both have a love of the outdoors, which led to a discussion about who we'd inherited that from; mum or dad? We both agreed it was dad. Mum has many qualities, but a love of the outdoors isn't one of them – she concreted over the garden in the house where Ruth grew up and chopped down a beautiful small leafed lime tree in the front garden that I remembered from my childhood.

I could hear them nattering and pondered about my family. Unlike Beth I grew up in Cumbria, dad worked at Glaxo Smithkline in Ulverston and we lived in Kents Bank. My mum taught at Alithwaite school. Even though me and my two brothers (one older, one younger) all went to the same school that mum taught at, and even though she drove there each day, she still made us walk. Obviously, as a child, I found that hugely unfair, but it wasn't the walk that scarred me – I actually didn't mind that – it was a big stinky field of cabbages that we had to walk past which is etched deep into my mind. I still don't like cabbage. I blame my mum.

Dad, on the other hand, walked, and walked and walked. We didn't have a car until I was well into my teens and we can both recall dad walking miles to work and to deliver church services (he was a Methodist Lay preacher). I also remember getting up early on family holidays to go for a walk with him before breakfast – probably the only reason Ruth didn't come along is because when I was an overly excited six-year-old up at the crack of dawn, she was a sixteen-year-old teenager and fond of her lie-ins.

Dad worked long hours during the week, but most weekends we'd go out walking in the fells. Mum and dad had a thing for collecting minerals so we'd often end up near one of the many old mine heaps in the county, sorting through the spoil heaps looking for interesting stuff; they still have a very impressive collection.

Down past Harrington there was a diversion on the footpath, but we soon found our way again. Thankfully the weather was a lot cooler and there was a lovely sea breeze coming in, making it one of the most pleasant hiking days so far. Our exhaustion was showing though and we had a fair few more stops than usual to shovel in tea and chocolate.

Ruth continued her walking when she was away at college in Crewe. 'When it all got a bit much, I went for a walk.'

Yes, I can definitely relate to that – walking has been my therapy on many occasions. Doctors should really be able to prescribe it instead of, or at least alongside, 'happy pills'; it's an awful lot cheaper and far better for you.

Ken's brother lives in Scotland and, one year, Ruth and Ken decided to head north and try out a two-week trip to Skye.

'To be honest, we were both a bit worried that there wouldn't be enough to do for two whole weeks but, by the end of it, we didn't want to come home.'

A love for Scotland and her many islands was born. Since then they have visited as many as they can and had recently returned from a two-week trip to Shetland.

> *My older brother isn't much into walking and the outdoors, but my younger brother is. We live miles apart now, but I remember going on a long hike with him all around Cumbria once. We stayed at a lot of Youth Hostels and I remember having to make the porridge each morning and doing our other chores. Hostels have gone upmarket now, it's no longer required to do the hoovering!*

My big sister has also beaten breast cancer. Twice. On the second occasion she underwent a course of chemotherapy as well as an operation and it was walking that helped her through. Although she couldn't get out and manage the long walks that she was used to, even on her toughest days she'd try and drag herself to the end of the garden.

Enjoying the sea breeze along the coastal path

'Just being outside made me feel a bit better.'

See? I told you doctors should be able to prescribe it.

While Ken and Steve wandered along, deep in conversation, me and Ruth had a wonderful time reminiscing about our childhoods. I remember walking back from Walsall with her on FA cup final day 1977 – Man Utd v. Liverpool. For some reason which eludes me, the ten-year-old me had decided that she was a Man Utd fan. We'd been shopping in Walsall while the match was on and I'd tried to keep up with it via the various TV shops around town. It was 0–0 when we started our walk home and 2–1 to Man U by the time we got back, with all three goals

All awash in the wash

being scored within five minutes in the second half. Funny what you remember, isn't it?

I wish I could tell you what me and Ken were talking about, but I honestly can't remember. It definitely wasn't football though as I never watch it. I think Ken does though. I do remember him saying he grew up near Kidderminster and he used to play in a band. Apparently, at the local working men's club, they'd sometimes play a set and some guy called Robert Plant would get up on stage and join in. Turns out yes it was *the* Robert Plant. He still lives near Kidderminster but doesn't play working men's clubs anymore.

A fine selection of local ales

By now we were descending down into Whitehaven where we had two beery visits planned. The first was to Gin & Beer It – a fantastic bar in the heart of town, owned and run by Louise and David Pegram, who serve the most fabulous array of gins, beers and belt-busting cold meat and cheese platters. Their influences come from the fact that they are both beer fans and met in France, where they discovered a shared deep and abiding love for good cheese. There will be no Dairylea triangles or boring, bland cheddars here. Absolutely all of their produce is carefully sourced and I can personally guarantee that if you eat there, then you won't need to eat again for a week or so …

The bar is quirky and welcoming and is gaining a well-deserved reputation as *the* place to go for local beer connoisseurs who come in to sample the ever changing selection of craft beers both on tap, and bottled. They've only been going since September 2018 but are already and integral part of the town and both love getting to know new people.

We sat around for an hour or so, enjoying a lovely natter and a few pints (only one each!) of their quirky beers. I'd opted for a sour cherry brew from Fell Brewery who we'd met earlier in the walk, it was very refreshing but easily the most unusual beer I'd sampled so far.

I really wanted to stay here for food. Their menu and big meaty platters looked fantastic, but Beth had us booked in somewhere else. It had better be good …

On to our next stop, this time for dinner. We were booked into The Vagabond down on the quayside, which was named in honour of Bob Dylan. Stefan, who now owns the bar, used to work for the previous owner who sold up and moved on four years ago. It's a snug and popular place with an extensive menu.

They stock a range of Cumbrian ales but told me about one occasion when they'd been unable to get Loweswater Gold for a period of time. It's one of the most popular beers in the county and, when people came in to order it, only to find they had none, they'd turn tail and leave, rather than sample something different. Thankfully, it's now back in stock.

Ok, all is forgiven, the food was decent and they had good beer.

'So, what's so special about Loweswater Gold then?' Ken asked, pint in hand.

Well, I'm glad you asked! It's brewed by Cumbrian Legendary Ales over near Hawkshead, and we'd been over to see them before we set off.

Roger and Helen Humphreys started the business up at Kirkstile Inn in Loweswater in 2003. They were keen to recognise the Cumbrian landscape in the names of their beers, hence Loweswater Gold. The beer was an instant hit and has gone on to become a Cumbrian classic. I have friends who don't believe their holiday up here has started until they've had a pint.

In 2009 they bought Cumbrian Legendary Ales and moved over to Hawkshead where the lovely Ian is now head brewer and Rachael looks after the business side.

The water for the beer comes from Levers Water and requires very little treatment to produce the crisp, clean, very drinkable Loweswater

Also served here!

Gold. It's the best-selling hand pumped beer in Cumbria and appeals to a broad spectrum of folks.

It's by far their best seller, something they take very seriously because getting consistency with beer isn't always easy. A change in weather can affect the taste of the hops, and a flood, or drought, can affect the quality of the water etc. So, like Jennings Brewery, these guys control what they can and keep a sample of their yeast in the yeast bank in London. As Ian says,

'Yeast is like a pet, you really have to look after it and treat it right, and make sure it doesn't get stressed.'

I think my next book should be 'Mindfulness for Yeast'.

Are you kidding me? You're on your own with that one.

All of these local breweries may be small, but between them they employ quite a workforce. Cumbria Legendary Ales employ eight people altogether and that's something we've seen repeated right across the county.

To be honest, I'm not sure that Ken was expecting quite such a detailed answer, but he was still awake, which I took as a good sign.

Resting on the quayside at Whitehaven

All too soon it was time to part company, we had a B&B to find, and they had a long drive ahead of them. We paused for a few photos down on the quay before going our separate ways.

I had really been looking forward to today and spending some time with my sister and I had thoroughly enjoyed it. We really must do it again next time I'm hauling a beer cask on a 138-mile hike.

We bid them farewell and began the long uphill walk to the B&B. Why were they always uphill? All I was craving now was some clean sheets and a good night's sleep. That's not too much to ask, is it?

Uphill she says. Not a small hill either. Nope. A flipping enormous one. And the Airbnb was right at the top. Of course it was. As we finally staggered onto the driveway of the place we were staying the owners pulled up in their car. We chatted for a while and it turns out they had been sitting two tables away from us in the pub where we'd just eaten and could have given us a lift up the great, big, enormous hill. I tried not to cry.

BREWERY: Cumbrian Legendary Ales

WEBSITE: cumbrianlegendaryales.com

BEERS: Loweswater Gold, Buttermere Beauty, Grasmoor Dark Ale

TOURS? No at present

TAP ROOM? No, but well stocked across the county

STOCKED: Extensively stocked in bars and shops across the county

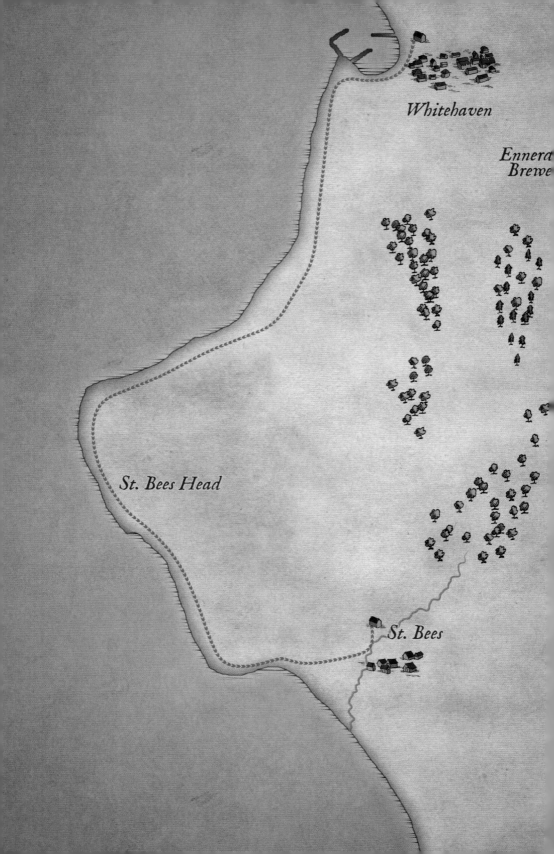

Whitehaven

Ennera
Brewe

St. Bees Head

St. Bees

We are family

 Start: Whitehaven Harbour

End: St Bees seafront

Distance: 6.8 miles/ 10.1KM

Terrain: Hard track, tarmac, overgrown cliff top path

Transportation: Train – stations at St Bees and
Whitehaven

OUR LIVES WERE REVOLVING around sleep; we desperately
needed it but weren't always getting it. Take last night, for
example. The digs had everything going for them; great location, small,
private annex behind a house on a quiet street, lovely lounge area and
a small but perfectly formed bedroom upstairs. We watched a bit of TV
in the lounge and I was looking forward to a lovely early night and a nice
long sleep.

Around 9:30pm I bid Steve 'goodnight' and headed upstairs. I got
into my night shirt (least stinky t-shirt) and sat on the edge of the bed.
'CRRREEAAKKK!' – not me, the bed (although, to be fair, it was a close
run thing!). It let out the loudest creak I had ever heard. I stood up
again. 'CRRRREEAAKKK!' My hopes of a quiet, peaceful night were fast
evaporating.

Bathroom duties completed I returned to bed. 'CRRREEAAKKK!' –
Every single time I sat, or shifted position, the noise was the same. It
went on all night, each time I rolled over the bed made such a racket
that it woke up both of us, and possibly several neighbours too. I was so
desperate for a good sleep that I could have cried. In fact I think I did; at
around 3am when I'd woken myself up for the dozenth time. I'd so been
looking forward to a lie it, and now I just wanted the night to be over
and us to be on our way again.

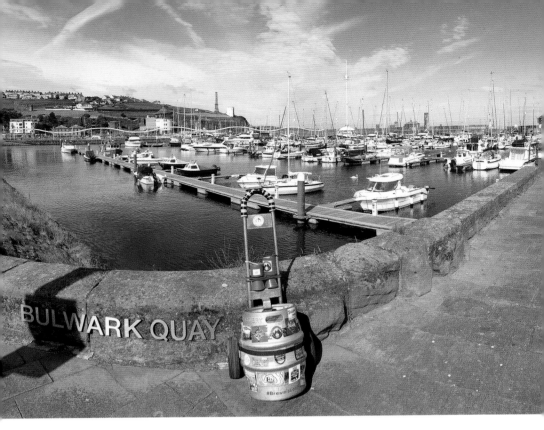

When your beer cask wants to go by yacht but you have a nice walk in mind

I heard the creaking, of course I did, but it was mainly on Beth's side of the bed. I jokingly suggested that it was perhaps due to that extra Mars bar she'd scoffed yesterday. It turns out my timing may have been a little off with that one …

It was times like this that made me wish I could drink caffeine. I've always been rather hyper and often struggle to sleep, so have been strictly decaf for many years now, but today I could have really done with a shot or two in the arm.

Beth on caffeine is like the Looney Tasmanian Devil; would have been handy flying that cask up them steep hills though. She also carries a couple of EpiPens with her – a couple of shots of adrenaline could have come in handy around about now too.

We breakfasted on some old packets of cereal we had lying around in our rucksacks and, while Steve whizzed off to get a couple of photos.

Taking in the sights around Whitehaven

The Candlestick, Whitehaven

I restocked our backpacks with goodies from Tesco before haring off to meet our walking companions for the day; Jodi, Emily and Emily from Ennerdale Brewery.

The thing that immediately strikes you about Ennerdale Brewery is that it is a family affair. It's not just the fact that dad started the brewery and now mum, children and in-laws work there, it's the fact that even the employees who are not related by blood are still treated like family. The warmth and love of being together hits you right from the start. In fact it took me most of the walk to figure out who was related to who. (Jody and one Emily are sisters and the other Emily joined to help out on a casual basis many years ago, but just can't seem to leave.)

I thought I might have offended them when we met. Beth was still buying snacks, and chatting to a fellow author she bumped into in Tesco (she didn't mention that part, did she? She can always find someone to natter to. 'I'm only popping out for ten minutes to get some milk' she says, then rocks up home an hour or so later), and I was worried about getting some nice photos before we set off. I saw Jody, Emily and Emily but shouted a quick 'hello' as I shot past to take photos around the harbour.

'We're happy to help you haul the cask,' they said. 'Unless you feel like you have to haul it the whole way for the book.'

Result!

Nope. Not at all. I know I'm supposed to say that the nicest thing about walking with different people was the fact that we made new friends and learned new and exciting things, but the reality is that new people thought that hauling the cask was a novelty and wanted to have a go, and we were quite happy to let them.

Our destination for the day was St Bees, seven or so miles over the cliffs and a pretty straightforward route: Keep the sea on your right at all times, and no nasty trading estates getting in the way to confuse us.

Those that know the area know that the first thing in our way was a very big, steep, hill. I love Whitehaven; it has a wonderful history and lots of magnificent views, so I was pausing every 50 yards or so to catch my breath and admire them.

> *I did do some pulling, then, at the top of the hill, when it was nice and flat, I whisked the cask away to get some photos as if I'd hauled it the whole way ...*

'So,' I ventured, as we hung around the Candlestick twenty minutes into the walk, and I considered diving into my lunch. 'I understand that you've not been at your new site long?'

Jodi looked puzzled. 'What makes you say that?'

'Well, when we've told folks that we're meeting you they've said that your "new place" is lovely.'

With Jodi and Emily from Ennerdale Brewery

Long grasses atop the cliff

'We've been there since November 2015,' she laughed.

Over the years I've lived up here one of the things I've had to get used to is the Cumbrian concept of time. I really should have known that 'new' could technically apply to anything up to ten years old, or possibly more. In the south of the county most people still haven't accepted the fact that they no longer live in Lancashire, and that boundary changed in 1974 ...

Originally from the north east, the family moved over to Cumbria when dad got a job at Sellafield. They lived in Ennerdale and launched the brewery in 2009 after dad's hobby of home-brewing got a bit out of hand. As well as a strong sense of family, they also have a strong sense of community and at both their old, and new, premises, they have always welcomed passers-by and locals in for a cup of tea and a natter.

Their first commercial beer was a blonde ale, then they launched their Black Sail bitter and today they have a steady range of regular beers, plus a number of seasonal guest ales.

Our conversation was interrupted by having to navigate the cask along some very overgrown tracks. 'Keep the sea on your right' might seem like a simple enough concept, but it was still hard picking out the footpath and, when it did appear, it was very narrow and overgrown and certainly not wide enough for a beer trolley. We all pitched in as we coaxed, cajoled and carried it along the cliff path. Eventually everything cleared and conversation could resume.

I nearly lost Beth a few times in the bracken, it was that high. Never seen anything like it. I'm sure it wasn't this high last time we came this way. Adders. What about adders? Don't they live in bracken? I was bitten by an adder once. Not in bracken but in our back garden when I was a kid. Hopefully the sound of the cask crashing through the undergrowth would scare them away.

Dave, the head brewer, loves to experiment. This was a common theme for all the breweries we met. They may be well known for one, or perhaps two, ales, but there's no room for complacency and every brewery seemed to have a head brewer keen to experiment and find new flavours. I had images of a mad scientist in long white lab coat and half-moon specs cackling as they mixed their potions on a dark, thundery night as flashes of lightening illuminated their foaming flagons of ale …

We paused in the sunshine for lunch before continuing on along the cliffs and down into St Bees. The second half the journey was a lot easier than the first on account of the fact that a) we could see the path and b) it was downhill.

Cheese savouries! Beth bought cheese savouries! I love a cheese savoury – grated cheese, onions and mayo. I think. I'm no chef. Beth does most of the cooking at home and she does make a nice sandwich. We also have a hiking motto: 'Don't diss the sarnie'. It all started after I tackled all 214 Wainwrights in 214 days in 2014. Beth's organised but I'm not and often went out without taking a proper packed lunch then couldn't understand why I was so tired in the afternoons. She claims sandwiches have magical healing powers, or something like that, either way I now always take a sandwich.

Stunning views over the Irish Sea

Down the hill to St Bees

Down in St Bees we dropped our rucksacks and cask at St Bees School, where we'd be spending the night, and jumped into Jodi's car for a lift to their 'new' site at Rowrah. What looks like a large industrial unit from the outside is, in fact, an incredibly welcoming tea room/ bar on the inside.

With Jodi, Emily and Emily in more blazing sunshine

Ready for some refreshments

Mum was busy serving behind the bar and overseeing the kitchen. Her cooking is the stuff of legend and, on one occasion, when they had some temporary help in the kitchen, the helper took the meat for the pie out of the slow cooker too early, so mum promptly it all back out of the pie and put it back into the slow cooker until it was properly done. When she's not baking the absolute finest steak and ale pies on the planet, she also experiments with 'sweets' gins and had an eclectic tray of

A welcoming tea room

'Drumsticks Gin', 'Pear Drops Gin' and 'Strawberry Shortcake Gin' available to sample.

I paused for a moment. Here I was, sat in a lovely tea room, surrounded by fabulous food, great beer, excellent gin, divine cakes and fantastic company. The sun was shining and we'd just enjoyed a glorious cliff-top walk with far reaching views. Tired and aching though I was, I also realised that I was incredibly flipping lucky. This was an epic adventure, and it wasn't over yet!

An excellent pint...

It really is a lovely place, and they treated us to the best steak and ale pie that I have ever tasted. I was so hungry too, my cheese savoury may have been magical but it was a long time ago. A massive slab of pie, mash and peas was just what I needed. Their Jack Daniels BBQ Chicken looked good too, but maybe next time. I wanted a pudding, I really did, but just didn't have room for one. I think the heat must really be affecting me. I never refuse puddings. Even when everyone else had keeled over and thrown

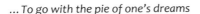

... To go with the pie of one's dreams

Some bottled offerings from Ennerdale Craft Brewery

in the towel, I can still eat a pudding. I began to worry that there was something seriously wrong with me.

As we sat and chatted over dinner a customer came over for a natter about mutual friends and family. It was just that kind of place; everyone knows everyone, but in a good way. Apparently their fireworks evenings are the stuff of legend with queues out of the door and beer and hotdogs as far as the eye can see. They also have an annual Barrel Run where competitors race, carrying a metal beer cask, from the brewery to the Fox and Hounds in Ennerdale. All the entry fee money goes to charity and kids can join in too – they're given a lightweight plastic 'pin' (smaller than a cask) to even things up a bit.

I was genuinely sorry to leave, and even sorrier that we didn't live an awful lot closer. This really did seem like the sort of place I would enjoy hanging out in, and I'm getting to that age where I don't enjoy hanging out in places where social etiquette dictates I shouldn't be in my pyjamas.

As long as you don't wear those big, furry, elephant pyjamas you like so much.

Back at St Bees school we took a stroll around the grounds as the light began to fade. I was beyond excited to be staying here. I adore rambling old buildings and, not only were we getting to stay the night here, we were also being treated to a full guided tour. We wandered around noticing small features and plaques that we could ask about the next day.

How lucky we are to be here!

The place has a very gothic feel to it with soaring spires and crenelated walls. Our room was tucked up in the eaves and, with the kids all having left on their summer hols just a few days earlier, we had the whole place to ourselves. Everything looked just perfect. I looked at my comfy, cosy, single bed and approached it slowly. I sat down gingerly on the edge, waiting ... but ... nothing! No creaking! No busy roads. No door slammers for miles around. Tonight there would be peace and quiet and tonight I would sleep a good, solid, ten hours, and lord help *anyone* who tried to disturb me!

My bed was comfy, and quiet, but I'm 6ft 4ins so always have to sleep at a bit of an odd angle when I'm in a single bed with a wooden end on it, so I can't hang my feet over the bottom edge. If you've ever seen the film Elf, where Will Ferrell is too big for everything around him – it's a bit like that sometimes.

The other annoying thing about single beds on opposite sides of the room is that I can't prod Beth when she snores. I did consider throwing things but knew how tired she was, so just left her to it. To be honest, after that enormous pie and a couple of beers, it wasn't long before I was asleep too. Not snoring though. I never snore.

BREWERY: Ennerdale Brewery

WEBSITE: ennerdalebrewery.co.uk

BEERS: Ennerdale Blonde, Honeycomb, Seven Bridges

TOURS? Yes, book via the webside

TAP ROOM? Yes, open 7 days a week and serves food, coffee and cake too!

STOCKED: Well stocked in local shops & bars

St. Bees

River Ehen

Egremont

Nethertown

River Calder

Sellafield

Seascal

Buzzing!

- **Start:** St Bees Seafront
- **End:** Seascale
- **Distance:** 8.3 miles/ 13.3KM
- **Terrain:** Sand, tarmac, hard track
- **Transportation:** Train – stations at Seascale and St Bees

I SLEPT! HALLELUJAH! Lots and lots of wonderful deep sleep in a cosy, quiet room. I really didn't want to leave my little cocoon, but the sun was shining and breakfast and a tour of the school awaited; I was good to go!

> *They had left us a huge breakfast and we had an enormous common room/kitchen all to ourselves. We both drank a couple of mugs of tea before filling our flasks. Then there was toast and cereal and then more toast again. Now the weather had cooled down a bit I was enjoying carbo-loading.*

Laurence Gribble was our guide for the tour – he's the Deputy Director for Full Circle who run the school and, I'll be honest, he looked way too young to be a deputy director, but that has nothing to do with him actually being too young and everything to do with my preconceptions. He's an ex-pupil which means he knows every nook and cranny of the place and also means that there's not a lot that the present pupils can get up to which he isn't already wise to, having probably done it himself.

The school was founded in 1583 and there's a list of the headmasters on the wall dating right back to day one. The school came into being after Edmund Grindal, Archbishop of Canterbury, rather rudely informed Queen Elizabeth I that this was 'the ignorantest part in religion, and most oppressed of covetous landlords of any one part of this realm.'

St Bees School

The first part of the school was built with stones robbed from the priory over the road. Well, I say robbed, it was really just an early example of re-cycling. The school was originally only open to locals, comprised of two stories and has the words 'Enter so that you may make progress' still visible over the original doorway.

Were people just shorter back then? I kept banging my head on the old door frames.

What is now the dining room was once the school room and, etched deep into the wooden panels around the room, are the names of past students; clearly a form of graffiti but today a lasting reminder of the boys who passed through the doors. One panel in particular was very thought-provoking; it contained the names of eight boys who had then gone on to lose their lives in World War One. Above the panel where they'd surreptitiously carved their names, no doubt, with much sniggering and bravado, there was a brass plaque commemorating their deaths, a ridiculously short number of years later. In total 987 'boys' served in World War One and 183 died, as did four of the masters.

Back in the day the school owned pretty much all of the land around St Bees and the annual rents from the properties were a useful income stream. Although that's no longer the case there is still an incredibly close bond between the school and the village.

It was founded as a Church of England school and, although it has a wonderful chapel, today they welcome all religions and take a holistic approach to teaching religion focusing on the history and geography of a region, as well as its religion, seeing as they're all inextricably linked.

I loved the old building and, while Beth was deep in conversation with Laurence, I was enjoying looking at the plaques on the wall. There was some pretty cool art too and I couldn't believe it was done by the pupils.

Over the years the school developed and grew, taking in boarders, adding wings and eventually, in the 1970s, opening its doors to girls as well as boys. In the foyer there's a cabinet full of trophies, but none of them are for academic achievement, instead they all celebrate sporting or other extra-curricular activities – Laurence was keen to show the school values everything about a person, not just their IQ. Even their entrance 'exam' isn't pass/ fail but an assessment of the starting point, strengths and weaknesses for each pupil.

I really liked that about the school. I'm not great in exams and it never seems fair that the kids who get on are usually the ones just good at taking exams. What about the ones who are good at art? Or cooking? Or brewing beer?

In 1987 a new sports hall and squash courts were added (because *everyone* was playing squash in the 1980s) and these, together with the original pool (the oldest school-owned pool in the country) were also open for the villagers to use too.

The school chapel

More recently the school closed in July 2015; they were full of students, but the finances were not adding up. As well as affecting the students, this closure had a colossal impact on the village – the local shop that kept the students supplied with sweets and snacks, the local cleaners, caterers, laundry service and the groundsman. Many of these local business also suffered as a consequence, but the local groundsman, whose father had been groundsman before him, said he just couldn't watch the stunning grounds go to rack and ruin and continued to work, every single day, for no money, just to keep everything looking beautiful.

I looked at the grounds. They were huge. Several football fields at least. I really didn't fancy mowing that lot – paid or unpaid.

In 2018 they reopened their doors to year 7 students and, in 2019, years 7, 8, +9 and 12. As an independent school they aren't tied to the National Curriculum and offer a 'Fusion Curriculum' which combines British and Chinese teaching methods. In China maths is usually the subject that kids enjoy most, but that's rarely the case in the UK, so there's clearly something we can learn from that (apart from maths!).

Our tour was nearing a close. We came back around to the front of the building and peered into two large outdoor courts.

'What do you think these are then?' asked Laurence.

We both looked around.

'Squash?'

'Nope.'

'Some sort of racketball?'

'Close, but no.'

'Somewhere to practise cricket in the dry?'

'Not quite.'

'Give up.'

'Eton fives'

'Eton what?'

Turns out Eton fives is a very curious game, similar to squash in many respects in that it's played in a three-sided court with a small ball, but there no rackets, only gloves, and the courts are an exact replica of a section of the outside of Eton College chapel where it all began. And I mean an exact replica – there's a step in the middle of the court and half

A selfie with Kate Wilson, supplier of ice cream and Kendal Mint Cake

a buttress jutting out on the left hand side. It's always played as doubles and there is no umpire, players are entirely self-governed and the rules of good sportsmanship always apply. How wonderfully British!

We bid farewell to Laurence, reclaimed our cask, and made our way to the beach. The weather was stunning; bright and sunny, but with enough of a sea breeze to keep us nice and cool. I believe there is a local by-law which dictates that anyone visiting St Bees beach has to stop and enjoy an ice-cream at Hartley's on the sea front, and I've never been one to break the law (or at least admit I have in a book!), so we sat in the sunshine enjoying our ice-creams and having a natter with my lovely friend Kate Wilson, who lives locally and had come along to offer some moral support. Seeing a friendly face along the way always made a big difference, especially when they paid for the ice creams and thrust slabs of Kendal Mint Cake into our hands to keep us going. Thanks Kate!

Kate turned up in a Subaru – me and Beth met, many years ago, because we both drove Subarus. We got rid of them a long time ago, but I still have a soft spot for them. Maybe if lots of people buy this book I can get another one?

Off we set along the beach. We'd checked the tide times and reckoned we had a good hour or so to make it down to the car park at the far end, where we could cut up onto the road for the rest of our trip, and we were right, mostly. We had plenty of time to make it and would have done so very easily if we hadn't stopped to take quite to many photographs along the way, meaning we had to haul the cask

A refreshing spot of brine about the undercarriage

over pebbles for the final stretch, not something either of us are keen to repeat!

> *She worries too much. We were fine. It was just a bit of shingle and the tide was miles away. Ish ...*

I'll be honest, road walking is by far the easiest way to walk with a cask, but it's really rather monotonous. We broke our journey in Nethertown where we enjoyed a beer in the shade (by this stage of the journey one or other of us was bound to have a bottle of beer stashed somewhere in our rucksacks), and our bottles of Ennerdale Blonde went down very nicely with a few bits of flapjack.

The horizon was dominated by Sellafield, but we also passed a couple of interesting older buildings along the way – the tower in Braystones, which was erected in 1897 to celebrate Queen Victoria's Diamond Jubliee, and the very lovely St Bridget's church in Beckermet (pronounced Beker-met), which is small, simple and really rather beautiful.

Braystones
Tower

St Bridget's,
Beckermet

A prickly gorse trail

You could definitely tell that there was a lot more money here. The houses in the villages were bigger and smarter. The cars were bigger too. I once got caught in a Sellafield rush hour when everyone piled out at the end of their shift. Because they're the only big employer around here you really notice it when a shift ends. I was up on a hill, in the middle of nowhere when dozens of cars came racing through.

I was getting annoyed with some of the rights of way around here though. To get to the church at Beckermet we had to walk around a HUGE loop of road, when I could see a perfectly good track cutting across a nearby field. Beth's really picky about that sort of thing so we walked all the way around. To be honest I can see her point, if I were the farmer, I'd be really annoyed if people kept cutting across my field, but the cask was heavy and I was tired.

Cask hauling here was nice and easy as we followed a popular cycle track, but every step took us closer to Sellafield with its curious collection of buildings. I've probably watched way too much science fiction in my time and, for deeply irrational reasons most likely relating to being psychologically scarred by Quatermass at a young age, I found our route around the perimeter rather disturbing.

All around the perimeter were vast fences, topped with barbed wire and 'Strictly Prohibited' notices, roughly every 50m or so. Two things struck me: firstly, surely the word 'strictly' was redundant? Has anything ever been 'occasionally prohibited, but actually we're pretty laid back about the whole thing'? I somehow doubt it.

I really don't trust nuclear power plants. How do you know it's not leaking? I was keen to get through this part as quickly as I could. Although the collection of buildings was definitely interesting.

Secondly, why so many signs? Are they worried that the area is surrounded with amnesiacs? Are folks likely to walk along the vast fences, see the signs, wander a little further, completely forget the sign they saw a few minutes earlier and have a crack at scaling the fence? Again, unlikely. Unless all that radiation does odd things to your mind ... We upped the pace.

Arriving into Seascale we dumped our cask in the hotel room (small room, freakishly large TV).

Small room, perfectly reasonably sized TV.

We returned to the benches outside to have a natter to Matt Legg, Senior Media Relations Manager for Sellafield. You may think it's a curious place to include, but the site has had a huge impact on the recent history of the region, and continues to do so and I had loads of questions I wanted to ask him.

Steve approaching Sellafield

I had a few questions I wanted to ask Matt too. Things like, would I glow in the dark now? Beth glared at me and I thought better of it.

We learned tons of fascinating stuff from Matt and, being a bit of a nerd, I could easily fill the rest of this chapter with it, but I will try to restrict myself to a few juicy bullet points.

- The building work began in 1947 and the plant was online in 1950. Today it would take roughly that long to get the permits sorted but, in 1947, we'd just won World War Two and, as a nation, we were massively confident, perhaps overly so ...
- The downside of that was that we rushed into things that we could just 'deal with later'. Now is later and they are still busy mopping up a lot of stuff from back then.

Another day, another cliff-top walk

- Seascale, the unassuming little seaside town where we were now stood, was once home to the very finest scientific minds in the country. They lived here while they built the power plant.
- Workington, just up the coast, was the first town in the world to have all its electricity produced by a nuclear plant.
- The plant was, and is, a source of immense local pride. In the current climate it's easy to forget that we led the world in this venture. Previously the region was known for coal mining – fathers had spent their lives down dark and dirty pits, and now their sons could work in clean, modern facilities. This was revolutionary.
- The plant employs roughly 11,500 people and it's the only local authority outside of London, where the average wage is over £40,000. (We'd noticed all the posh houses in the nearby villages we'd wandered through).
- All the beaches are regularly checked for radioactive waste. Something we'd see the next morning from the hotel window as we had breakfast.
- The site is currently decommissioning, it's going to take around 100 years, but they are planning for that already by investing heavily in other technologies and education to provide employment in the area. For example they're converting the old bus station in Whitehaven into a technological/ digital hub to create new skills and employment.

Honestly, I have pages and pages of more notes, I was truly fascinated by it all, but you're probably beginning to nod off, so I'll leave it there.

Nothing about glowing in the dark though, was there?

With nowhere to eat in town (it was late on a Sunday evening) we grabbed a couple of pot noodles from the corner shop, added a pint of Loweswater Gold from the hotel bar and curled up in bed to watch Everest on TV. I looked at Steve and I could see what was running through his mind.

'Don't go getting any ideas – remember how tricky Helvellyn was.'

I think his smile was meant to reassure me. It didn't.

I know we can't go to Everest. Don't be silly. I'm just Googling flights for fun. May is a good time of year for it. Apparently. Not that I'm thinking of it. And we'd need skis or something for the trolley.

Oooohh – what if we just climbed the same height as Everest, but around the Lake District? We could do it for the launch. Or another book or something. I would have mentioned it to Beth but she was asleep already.

Boot

Devoke Water

River Esk

La'al Ratty

Muncaster Castle

Ravenglass

River Irt

Eskmeals Dunes

Drigg Dunes

Seascale

La'al rascal

Start: Seascale

End: Ratty Arms, Ravenglass

Distance: 5 miles/ 8KM

Terrain: Sand, tarmac, hard track

Transportation: Train – stations at Seascale and Ravenglass

AS WE BREAKFASTED, we watched the Sellafield truck taking samples off the beach, just like they said they would. And no alarms went off, so we took that as a good sign, packed up our gear and sauntered out into the sunshine. Our walking date for the day was the inimitable Sally of 'Sally's Cottages' and we loitered in the sunshine awaiting her arrival and enjoying the views, with both of us commenting that we couldn't believe it was nearly all over. There were mixed emotions; we were having an absolute blast, but were both completely knackered and, if I'm brutally honest, I was quite looking forward to walking somewhere without a beer cask in tow and sleeping in the same bed for more than two nights in a row.

I never took my eyes off that truck. I was just waiting for the alarms to go off, but they didn't. Not sure what I'd have done if they did, but I was watching. Just in case.

The thing is, on social media it probably looks like a lot of fun, glamorous even, but those are just the snapshots; the rest of the time we were just two sweaty hikers, inexplicably lugging a beer cask along the road and, I might add, getting some very odd looks in the process.

Glamorous? Last night we ate Pot Noodle in bed. Living the dream!

Sally arrived bang on time. She doesn't so much have a presence as a gravitational pull. I honestly couldn't believe she'd agreed to come with us; she is the multi-award-winning head of Cumbria's most popular holiday cottage company and we were just two nutters with a beer cask – and it wasn't even full. Still I've always admired her and was absolutely delighted to have the opportunity to get to know here a little better.

Two lunatic women. Great. Beth really doesn't need anyone putting any more mad ideas into her head. (Written by the man who is still considering dragging a cask up Everest.)

Like the previous day we decided to leg it along the beach and race the tide in – not as irresponsible as it sounds as there were plenty of escape routes. Time to get the basics out of the way along the first stretch.

Again, we had loads of time. We'd have had even more if there hadn't been quite so many selfies. Though a photo of the beer cask chilling on a hammock had to be done.

Sally was born and raised in Eskdale and, as a child, had always been under the impression that there were only three career options available to her – hospitality, farming or Sellafield. It was only when she went away

Just chillin'...

to university in Durham that she realised that there was a whole world out there with a whole range of opportunities. Before she went to Durham she thought that being a banker meant sitting behind the counter at Natwest and giving out sweets to kids. Even so, after three years studying monkeys, apes and various tribal customs in her anthropology degree, she came back to Cumbria and started her career in tourism.

We made it to the car park in plenty of time and, as I was in charge of navigation for the day, I offered a couple of options. There was a ford marked on the map, so I suggested we go and see if it was passable for folks on foot. It was only a short detour to check and, if that failed, there was another, slightly longer route we could try, over a packhorse bridge.

We aimed for the ford. We reached the ford. We quickly realised that unless we wanted to wade through three feet of slimy mud, or managed to flag down a passing tractor, we weren't getting across the ford. I wandered off to double check another part of it and, by the time I wandered back, Sally had used the mud to daub war paint on her face, which stayed there for the rest of the day. Sally is nuts. I like Sally.

It took us way too long to decide not to, we were tempted. It was only the first part that 'may' have been deep. With Beth as our 'bog buddy'* and me and Sally wielding a large branch, we would have been fine. Though it only just occurred to me, I don't think we thought about Casky.

*Bog Buddy – person sent on ahead in boggy conditions to check if it's safe. If they sink, or fail to return, best take a different route.

Sally, painted for action

We Googled a picture of the pack horse bridge we were aiming for and were all mightily impressed with what we saw, then we looked closer and realised that we were looking at a bridge of the same name in deepest Derbyshire ... Undaunted, and with no other options, we journeyed on.

Sally has clearly always had an entrepreneurial streak. Her dad used to tend pigs and sheep on their hill farm, before realising that to stay afloat, they would have to diversify. So he put a tap in the corner of one of their fields and proclaimed it was now a campsite. When campers started arriving, they gave constructive feedback pointing out that they'd quite like a toilet so he hastily put one in and things grew from there.

Young Sally, only being around five or six at the time, immediately saw an opportunity. Working in cahoots with her sister she would walk over the fells to the local shop and buy a bag of 1p sweets, then sell them to the campers for 5p each As she got older she took on chores around the site, cleaning the loos and keeping everything looking spic and span.

That got me thinking; what if I filled a cask with beer and dragged it to remote campsites to sell pints to weary campers? Or I could find all the wild campers on the fell tops? What about in the winter? Could I get an insulated cask full of hot chocolate? Could I use a drone to air lift in beer to wild campers? I began hatching plans and wasn't paying much attention to the route.

By now we'd navigated our way through Drigg and down to Holme Bridge where we found an incredibly pretty and unspoilt packhorse

Drigg Holme packhorse bridge over the River Irt, definitely in Cumbria

bridge. It was absolutely gorgeous; quiet and peaceful with a gentle stream running underneath. Take that Derbyshire.

We managed to find a wonderful old route through the fields down into Saltcoats before winding our way into Ravenglass. A much shorter than usual walk but I wasn't complaining, especially as Sally had insisted on hauling the cask the entire way. It seems our original concept of 'let's haul a cask around Cumbria' had evolved into more of a 'let's persuade lots of people to walk with us and they can haul the cask around Cumbria for us' reality. Works for me.

> *Are you sure I didn't haul it at all that day? I'm sure I must have. I wouldn't have let Sally drag it the whole way while I made plans for my beer laden drones, would I? 'Chocs Away' – remote hot chocolate delivery for weary hikers. I made a mental note to contact Dragon's Den as soon as we got home.*

As we sat with a round of pints in the Ratty Arms, awaiting our train up the valley, I delved more into Sally's past – how had she ended up running Sally's Cottages? By accident, it turns out … she'd continued working her entrepreneurial magic as an adult and had followed a natural progression from sweets to property. She started by renting a house for £500 per month and then sublet it to visitors for £500 a week.

It worked beautifully and it wasn't long before other people asked her to help them rent their cottages out too. Other people began asking her to take on their properties too, and it's all just grown from there. She created a website portal for bookings, sorted out the cleaning and developed an excellent reputation for customer service which is still at the heart of everything she does.

Well, that and doing other ridiculous things, like leaping off a jetty into Derwentwater dressed in gold hotpants. Or

*Must be time
for a pint*

dragging an office desk and chair to the top of Blencathra because it would look good in a photo (she was right, it did!).

She also has a habit of diving into situations that would terrify most of us.

'I once took on a cottage and then took bookings for it, but two weeks before the first guests arrived, it still had no internal walls.'

'Why would you do something like that?' I asked, my stress levels rising at the thought.

'I like working to deadlines,' she laughed. 'And anyway, things always work out.'

It turns out she works with her husband Rob and he's become a dab hand at, amongst other things, building walls really quickly. Our conversation was very reminiscent of the one I'd had with Debs on our way to Skiddaw House – the self-employed are usually a little more gung-ho when it comes to launching into ridiculous ventures.

We were all overly excited at our trip on La'al Ratty – officially the Ravenglass and Eskdale Railway. It's one of the iconic visitor attractions in the Lake District but, you know how it is, when something's on your doorstep you don't visit it as often as you should. I'd honestly thought that Sally would make her excuses and leave at this point, but not a

Excited big kids about to get on La'al Ratty

bit of it, she was as giddy as we were at the thought of an afternoon chuffing along the Eskdale valley.

There was a life-sized cardboard cut-out of the queen in the bar, so we had to get a photo. A month or so earlier me and Beth had guided the Duke and Duchess of Cambridge (yes, Will and Kate) on a walk around Ullswater. That was weird. I remember hearing Beth trying to explain William about hiking around Cumbria with a beer cask. I'm not sure they'll be asking us to guide royalty again. Still, at least we didn't end up in the Tower.

It was back in 1915 that the line as we see it today opened, although the original railway had been built in 1873 to shift iron ore from up in the valley, down to the coast, before gradually expanding to take on passengers. That line closed in 1913, due to a drop in demand, but it was reopened in 1915 with completely re-laid track and new engines. There is a fascinating history of La'al Ratty (Little Railway) in the station at Ravenglass.

This is a fabulous little steam train ride definitely one to do when you are on your Lake District holiday. As is the Haverthwaite steam line, oh, and a journey along the Cumbrian coastal line over its many estuary viaducts. In fact, you can also do the coastal line via steam train too. To be honest, I don't know what we were doing hauling a beer cask all this way, we could have just taken the train the whole way ...

I'd had no clue at the start of the day, but we were spending a day dragging Sally along memory lane. In her twenties she used to drink in

The best seat was reserved for Casky, of course

Showing off some of the stickers accumulated along the way

the Ratty Arms with her friends, many of whom worked on the railway, and they would occasionally sneak a train out in the middle of the night and take it up to the top of the valley and back. I was properly jealous of that – imagine a trip on La'al Ratty under the stars!

As we made our way up the valley our conversation was regularly interrupted by someone who knew Sally spotting her and waving, or Sally excitedly pointing out the house she grew up in, or the barn where she got married.

We stayed on all the way to the top at Dalegarth station before heading back down again. Me and Steve had to hop off early to find our accommodation and Sally was heading all the way back down to Ravenglass. She point blank refused any money or offer of a taxi and was quite

An action shot!

happy to walk all the way back to Seascale. She was rapidly becoming one of my favourite people.

We got off at Fisherground Station and waved goodbye until the train chuffed out of sight. The campsite we had to walk through to reach the road was the very one where Sally had cleaned the loos and sold sweets to the campers. As we made our way towards the pub and our bed for the night my phone pinged, it was Sally:

'When I got off in Ravenglass I bumped into someone I know who's giving me a lift back to Seascale. Hurrah!'

Sally was right again. Things do always work out.

The room was pretty basic, but clean, but there was no chance of hauling Casky up the tight, narrow, staircase, so we had to leave him in the bar. That's one of the fab things about Cumbria, and especially the more remote parts, you can just leave something like that in a bar without much fear of it 'walking'. Not that Casky was a 'thing' any more – we had bonded and I would have been gutted if anything had happened to him. I woke in the night worrying a little, but resisted the urge to tiptoe downstairs and check on him.

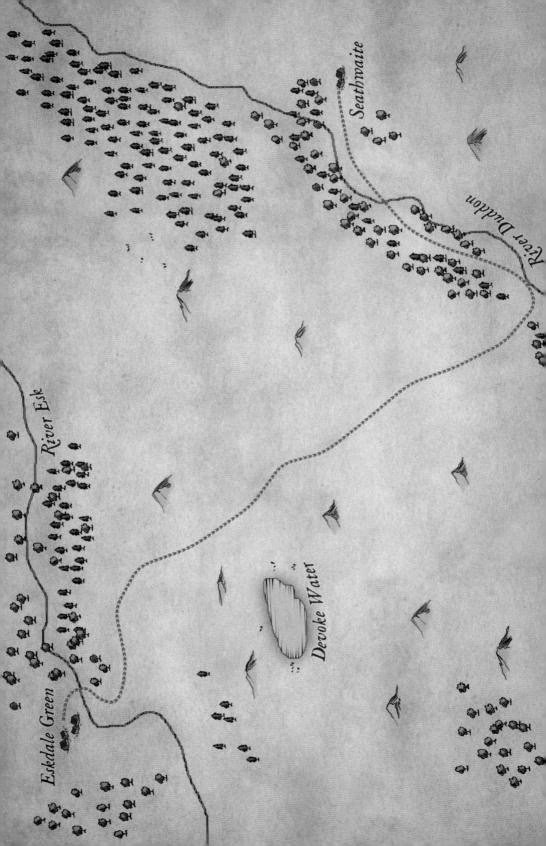

Seathwaite

River Duddon

River Esk

Eskdale Green

Devoke Water

Raining it in

- 🛢 **Start**: Eskdale
- 🛢 **End**: Seathwaite
- 🛢 **Distance**: 6 miles/ 9.6KM
- 🛢 **Terrain**: Mostly tarmac
- 🛢 **Transportation**: Not available

'JONTY'S A CHARACTER.'

Several people had told us this when they'd found out we were staying at the King George IV last night, and they were all right. Jonty *is* a character. He's the sort of man that fills a room. You could never be unsure whether Jonty was at an event, you would just know. His stature is imposing, his voice booming, and his gestures expansive. He's not 'like' anyone else; he is, simply, Jonty.

It's also important to catch him in a good mood. We'd been warned about that too. When we'd arrived last night he was brisk, almost brusque, and not particularly in the mood for a natter. To be honest, that suited us both fine as we were exhausted and valued a big plate of food over an hour or so of witty banter.

At breakfast time 'brusque' Jonty had been replaced by 'charming host' Jonty and nothing was too much trouble. We chatted about local beers as he furnished us with a quite splendid breakfast. He is passionate about beer and especially passionate about smaller breweries. The ceiling behind his bar is absolutely covered with beer mats and pump clips for the many hundreds of beers that he has served at one time or another.

As with many of the pubs we visited, it's pointless telling you what they have on tap as that can vary from week to week. In fact, that's one of the challenges for the local brewers. Having local pubs that

The King George IV Inn, Eskdale

support local breweries is, indeed, a fantastic thing, but it also brings in an element of inconsistency for the brewers. One week they may be 'on tap' in six local pubs, the next week just two and, the week after that, ten.

To help even things out most of the breweries aim to bottle their beers so they can a) supply supermarkets (more of that in a minute) and b) still be stocked in a bar, even if they're not on tap. Everyone we met, apart from Grasmere Brewery, got their bottling done at the same place in Cockermouth – they must love the micro-brewery boom in the county.

When it comes to supermarkets, things get tricky. Bottles need to have a shelf life stamped on them so brewers need to know how long the beer will be 'good' for in the bottles. The problem is that this can be affected by the way it's stored. Most pubs understand how to look after beer, but your average supermarket shelf stacker, most likely, does not. Perhaps a delivery has been left in hot sunshine for a few hours after it arrives, or left next to a heater, or anything else that could affect the flavour. That's a big fear for brewers because you could then pick up a bottle of their beer off the shelf, try it, hate it and vow never to touch that brand again, not because it's a bad beer, but because it's been badly stored – something the brewer has no control over.

Jonty was racing out to a meeting and disappeared off as soon as breakfast was done, but not before thrusting two enormous slabs of flapjack into our hands. I added Jonty to my 'nice' list.

For the first time in the hike, the weather had turned and, to be honest, neither of us was that upset about it. Yes, the blazing hot sunshine had made for some glorious photos and amazing views, but we were both fed up of being baking hot, sticky and sweaty. Way back at Crumble Cottages on night one, when I'd decided to ditch my waterproof trousers, I had been concerned that perhaps I'd need them, but now I was very glad I'd left them far behind. Today was grey and 'mizzley' but still warm so although my trousers would get wet, I'd be quite glad of it and, anyway, they'd dry pretty quickly too.

At least it was just light drizzle. Well, it alternated from mizzle to drizzle and then back again. It was nicer to be cooler for once, though wouldn't have liked it chucking it down and cold. I had to think long and hard weighing the odds (and literally weighing) whether I would need to wear gloves holding the metal cask handle all that way or have cold wet hands. I opted for reduced weight.

We set off. Today would be all road and a day of two halves. Half of it uphill and the other half down again. As we plodded along a motorbike pulled up alongside us, it was the other guests from last night's hotel.

Wait, what's that, a rain jacket?

They say romance is dead...

'Sorry, we didn't twig earlier,' they shouted through their helmets as they deposited some money into our collecting tins before racing off again, Our tins were now really quite heavy, which was obviously good for Mountain Rescue, but not so good for us ...

We recycled a couple of sandwich bags over the tops of the tins – don't want all those notes getting wet and filling up with water weighing me down even more.

At the top of Birker Fell we took a detour over to Devoke Water, said to be the largest tarn in Cumbria. The conditions were not great, the continuous drizzle had been joined by a stiff breeze, and I could not have been happier. I was cold. Actually cold! The lovely folks at 'The Outdoor Guide' had given me a lovely down jacket to wear on the walk and for once, I could actually wear it. Grinning inanely, I slipped it on, zipped it up, and pulled the hood over my head.

'You're really weird, you know that?' said Steve, as he watched me.

'Yeah, well, you knew that when you married me.'

We walked to the edge of the tarn, admired what there was of the view, then took a few photos before returning to the road.

A little further along a car pulled up alongside us, we readied ourselves to explain our story – we had it down to about 30 seconds now, and were well used to the odd looks. This time we didn't need to, the couple had seen us at St Bees and again at Fisherground Campsite the day before, where they were the wardens.

Spectacular, even in a mizzle

They explained that a few years earlier they had both left their jobs to walk from John O'Groats to Land's End to raise money for charity. It was a life changing experience for them and they never went back to their old lives, instead they toured Europe in a camper van and now look after campsites and travel the rest of the time. They gave us a donation before heading off. There really are so many interesting people in the world, but we're usually too busy, or self-conscious, to chat and find out.

We spotted a suitable spot to pause for tea and Jonty's flapjack – it was quite boggy terrain so perching spots were few and far between, but we found an old bridge along a farm tack and wolfed down a good half a slab each. (It really was a HUGE piece of flapjack – definitely Jonty sized!)

By now we'd crested the top of the hill and were heading down into the next valley when I spotted a sign: 'Cake Cupboard'. Oh I liked the sound of that! It turns out we'd discovered the Crosby Cake Cupboard (find them on Facebook, they are ACE!). You know how you can often find eggs, or honey, or sometimes jam, in a cupboard at the side of the road? Well, we'd discovered cake, and plenty of it too! I opened the door to be greeted with several shelves of muffins and assorted tray bakes. I'm not usually a very 'cakey' person and really don't have a sweet tooth but, by this stage of the hike, I would have willingly chugged a bag of sugar to keep me going.

Not only was there cake, but there was also a seating area; a few weeks later they were to open a cake hut with hot drinks and cakes for the weary traveller. I remember it so vividly; I selected a pack of two

An excellent innovation: the home-made cake cupboard

summer fruits and dark chocolate muffins and, the moment we bit into them, it was clear that they had come out of the oven just a few hours earlier. They were utterly divine – light, fluffy, and positively perfect in every single way. I didn't want to leave. I wanted to sample them all. It was an utterly brilliant idea, perfectly executed, and I sincerely hope they go from strength to strength.

Steve somehow managed to drag me away and we plodded downhill towards Seathwaite.

> *Wait a second, I dragged you away?! Me and cake, and I dragged you away?! Let me get this right. You who 'isn't very cakey' wanted more and me, 'Mr Cake monster' dragged you away?! Clearly I was having a momentary lapse of reason.*

At the bottom of the hill we turned left for the two mile walk into the village. I'd been hoping for a nice, flat, valley floor, but it was surprisingly undulating, which, in my now borderline delirious state, led to me proposing the idea of Brewers Loop – The Musical. Clearly I'd had far more sugary snacks than I was used to. I began rewriting the words to Les Miserable, turning 'One Day More' into 'One Hill More'. It could work – really it could …

'One hill more

Another day, another cake for me,

This never-ending road to chippy tea

Those men have said the weather's fine

And I must be in bed on time,

One hill more …'

Or perhaps not …

Video available on request.

As we plodded on, me singing, Steve trying to pretend he wasn't with me, we heard a large van approach from behind so stepped into the side of the road. The van stopped, it was Andrew from Fell Brewery on his way to make a delivery to the very pub we were staying in that night.

'Want a lift?' he asked, winding down the window and grinning.

'Yes, yes, YES!' screamed the voice in my head. There was another mile to go, and we were knackered.

Me and Steve looked at each other. We'd got this far without 'cheating' and weren't about to start now.

'No, thank you,' we muttered, trying to muster our most sincere smiles. After a brief chat about our adventures since we'd seen him he zoomed off, only to zoom back past us again on his way out of the valley, tooting and giving us a cheery wave.

I'm not saying we were in any way delirious, but, somehow, we also got onto the subject of adding 'sweat gutters' to the inside of waterproofs for hot rainy days – you know, those days when it's pouring down outside so you have to wear your waterproofs, but it's so hot that before long it's 'pouring down' inside your waterproofs as well. I'm really not sure how they'd work, but I'm not dismissing it as a completely ludicrous idea just yet …

To be honest this is our usual level of conversation when we go out hiking. Well, it's where we get all our crazy ideas from.

Seathwaite is a tiny village and the owners of the B&B where we were staying had also once been the owners of the pub, so we were lucky enough to find out a bit about the local history. There's documentary evidence for the pub all the way back to 1580, and it's really not changed a lot, but I mean that in a good way. The flagstone floors are superb and the thick, uneven walls are fresh and clean but not over modernised.

Dorothy and William Wordsworth once stayed in the pub, presumably with the express intention of visiting Seathwaite – unlike the hundreds of visitors who arrive in the village every single year who are actually looking for Seathwaite Farm and the start of the climb to Scafell Pike. As the crow flies it's ten miles between the two places but, as the car drives, it's over 40 miles. People simply plug 'Seathwaite' into the SatNav and follow where it leads, without checking if there's more than one Seathwaite.

It's bad enough if you're driving and have to add another hour to the route before you reach your start point, but there have been a few occasions when walkers have arrived in the village having parked at the correct Seathwaite, got themselves to the top of Scafell Pike, and then, somehow, managed to walk all the way down to the wrong Seathwaite. That's a very expensive cab ride …

Ok, we were tired, but we were nearly at the end of our epic adventure!

The valley is home to one of the newest, and smallest, micro breweries. Logan Beck Brewery is based just along the valley and, as they describe themselves, 'The beer is brewed in a barn by a man with a designer beard, a man with a proper beard and a man with no beard at all.' All the water for the beer comes straight out of Logan Beck, one of the tributaries for the River Duddon, and is the perfect starting point for their small, but growing, collection of beers.

Alex Douglas set up Logan Beck Brewing in October 2018, having worked behind the bar for the previous seven years and helped at the Foxfield brewery for four years before starting his own. Their main beer, Silver Lining, is absolutely packed full of flavour. Being small, they can be hard to find in pubs, but they make regular appearances at local beer festivals and are definitely one to watch!

We'd walked, we'd eaten, we'd drunk beer, now all I needed was a bed for the night. Fortunately our B&B was within a few wobbly paces of the pub so it wasn't long before I was snoozing away, dreaming of our final day of hiking and my very own bed again in just 24 hours' time.

You wanted more cake and I dragged you away?!

BREWERY: Logan Beck Brewery

WEBSITE: facebook.com/LoganBeckBrewery/

BEERS: Silver Lining, Prime

TOURS? No

TAP ROOM? Not at present

STOCKED: Limited stockists, often make an appearance at local beer festivals

Whose turn is it now?

Seathwaite

River Duddon

River Lickle

Broughton
in Furness

Foxfield

Final flocking day

Start: Seathwaite, Duddon

End: Prince of Wales, Foxfield

Distance: 8 miles/ 13KM

Terrain: Tarmac and hard track

Transportation: Not available

I WOKE AT AROUND 7am. Actually, that's a lie, I was woken at 7am by the rain thundering onto the Velux window. I'd also been woken at around 1am by the only other guest in the B&B hammering on the front door and ringing the bell to be let in after a late night out visiting friends camped nearby, then crashing and banging her way up to her room. Only one other guest and they still woke us up.

This was our last morning. The last day of a hike that had been six months in the planning. It seemed quite surreal. How did I feel? Exhausted mainly, not quite as tired as the start of day one, and certainly a lot less stressed, but really quite chuffed that we'd done it. It had been a lot of fun walking with Steve, proof that it's handy if you marry your best mate. We'd had a lot of laughs and very few fallings out. I wondered about all those people who'd said that it would 'test a marriage' and hoped they were ok.

Everything about this B&B was neat and precise, and that included breakfast, with the eggs, bacon etc. all neatly arranged on the plate. On the very rare occasions that I've attempted to make a full cooked breakfast things have been hurled onto the plate amid much cursing and smoke. Perhaps life as a B&B proprietor was not for me ...

Thankfully the rain eased over breakfast and had slowed to a steady drizzle by the time we left. There was an easier road route back out of the valley but it was the final day and I was in no mood to compromise.

Rocky. Need we say more

'It'll be fun!' I said as we trundled to the gate at the start of our climb.

Around half way up the climb that whole 'testing the marriage' part kicked in as we slipped, slithered and swore over rocks to the top of the pass.

'It'll look good in the book!' I said.

So, there it is, five lines in the book for a good 90 minutes of scrambling and swearing up the 'fun' route. Was it worth it? You decide.

The lovely Wednesday Walkers

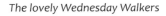

The rain gradually became mist and then stopped altogether as we crested our last major hill and headed down into the neighbouring valley. We encountered a rambling group on our way down – the Wednesday Walkers – who were very generous with donations before vanishing into the mist.

As we neared the road we spotted a cave on our right, and neither of us can resist a good cave! We nipped in for a bit of a nosey around, and probably breached several dozen health and safety guidelines in the process. This was clearly an old man-made mine and was the perfect spot for a few atmospheric photos of the cask. Armed with just a couple of head torches and the lights from our phones, some deft teamwork was needed to get the light just right for the pictures, but we did it and, I have to say, we're both rather pleased with the results.

The route was pretty straight forward apart from one section that involved plummeting through neck-high bracken and brambles to reach the old railway track into Broughton-on-Furness. At 6ft 4 Steve's neck is a lot higher than mine, and even he struggled.

Casky in a cave

He went that way...

At one point all I could hear was Beth's voice from deep inside a large bramble bush. It was a surreal experience. I couldn't see her at all. It was as if the bush was talking to me, telling me to follow it. I was very tired. I may have been hallucinating.

As we rambled along the track to the village, we passed a dog walker who paused for a natter, a donation and a recommendation to stop at The Manor for a pint, which we did.

'Is it Cumbrian?'

'It's beer, drink it.' I answered, slumping into the chair next to him. One final push and we were done, but I was fading fast.

As refreshed as we were ever going to be, we pushed on to our finishing point at The Prince of Wales in Foxfield. Why there? Why not. We had to finish somewhere and this place is a bit of a local legend. But the most welcome sight awaited us in the carpark before we even made it into the pub – our fabulous friend Diane Hannah, co-founder of The Herdy Company was right there, in the car park, with an enormous Herdy. I hugged them both. Herdy first, of course.

We staggered into the Prince of Wales who, due to a communications slip-up, had zero idea who we were, but could not have been more friendly and welcoming. Di got the beers in as I sat at a nearby table trying to assimilate what we'd just achieved.

I'd finished pulling the cask. I'd done it. We were at the final destination. I was happy and sad but mainly I was exhausted. Di put a pint and some peanuts down in front of me and I munched my way through them as Beth and Di chatted. I wondered if Casky needed anything; he'd had a

With our friend Diane, and possibly the most deserved pint supped in the whole of Cumbria that day

long journey too. There were a lot of wonderful smells wafting from the kitchen and I could happily have eaten whatever it was they were cooking.

We got to nattering and I realised how little I knew about how Di and Spencer (her husband) came to start the whole Herdy thing. Turns out they are college sweethearts (awww!) and met at Leicester Polytechnic 35 years earlier. Diane lived in Rochdale while Spencer was a Bolton lad and in 2002 they bought a small house in the Lake District which they planned to use at weekends, but they loved it so much that just a year

A fair few at Foxfield

Greetings from Herdy!

later they moved up permanently. Of all the incredible things Diane told me about her life and achievements, I was most impressed with her story of getting Fiat Panda up and over Hard Knott Pass just two weeks after passing her driving test. Impressive!

By now they'd started their own design company and in 2005 went on holiday to Helsinki to celebrate a milestone birthday. While they were there they noticed how wonderful slick, clean and modern designs of many of the gift shops. The seeds were sown and in 2007 Herdy came into being. Their focus has always been on impeccably designed products, sourced as ethically as possible and produced to the very highest of standards. Their shops are crisp, bright and clutter free and always an absolute joy to visit.

Herdy has attracted a whole army of 'superfans' and Diane and Spencer work hard to get the balance between fun and serious business, just right.

Whilst many of their products are made in the UK and they support small businesses and producers across the country, some of their products are made by responsible businesses in Sri Lanka which offer very poor communities the chance to learn new skills and earn a proper income. In Easter 2019, when the Sri Lanka church bombings occurred, killing 259 people and injuring 500 more, one of their workers was caught up in it. Her daughter was injured and her husband and mother-in-law

Ulverston Canal Foot

All smiles at the end of our journey

were killed. It was clear that this had affected Diane, whose firm view is that people are people, wherever they are, and the total inclusivity of the Herdy philosophy runs through everything they do.

As we enjoyed our beers Linda and Stuart, owners of The Prince of Wales, came over to join us and the banter and conversation spread to the rest of the pub, this was turning into a mini party!

I thought about joining in the conversation, but Beth seemed to have it all under control, so I focused on my beer and peanuts.

As well as running the pub Linda and Stuart have also been brewing their own beer on site since 1997. The place is far from slick and modern; instead it is quirky and homely, with the smell of fresh, home-cooked, no-nonsense food wafting from the Linda's kitchen. They'd both worked in pubs before deciding that they could make better beer themselves, so they did, and the pub is one of those which is incredibly popular with locals in the know, but doesn't generally attract many visitors.

They were also the only other place, apart from Grasmere Brewery, to make cider. Not a lot of folks outside the county are aware of the fact that South Cumbria is home to a large number of heritage orchards and the South Lakes Orchard Group (SLOG) members regularly donate apples to the Prince of Wales and are 'paid' in cider.

We could do that – we have apple trees! Each year I make my own cider, but it never tastes like anything you get in a pub. Maybe I could start my own business. Everyone else in the county seems to be brewing something, may as well join in! Otherwise I could brand it as apple vinegar. Alcohol wise, it's pretty lethal so maybe there is a market for organic drain cleaner.

Their brews are infamous and they continually make up their own recipes, but don't go looking for them anywhere else, you'll only find their beers in their pub. They're not after world domination, they just want to make good beer and enjoy it with all the regulars who continually stream through the door. A crowd was building at the bar so Linda and Stuart bid us farewell and returned to their customers. (Update: At the time of writing, the Prince of Wales is on the market so things may well have changed by the time you read this, which is a shame because as well as brewing lovely beers, it's a unique piece of local Cumbrian history.)

'Any interesting beer stories?' I asked Diane.

'Well, there was the time that Spencer lived in a really run-down house whilst we were at college. The University gave the guys sharing the house a few quid towards paint to do it up, but they blew the lot on home brew.' She laughed. 'Better not put that in the book.'

'Your secret is safe with me,' I smiled. (To be fair I did get her permission to use it.)

It was time to leave. Time to finally go home. The pub is directly opposite Foxfield railway station and large printouts of the latest timetables adorn the walls, but Diane was having none of it and insisted on giving us a lift.

I wondered just how cheeky I could be.

'Could we take a small detour along the way?' I asked.

'No problem at all!'

Where was she taking me now?

The final pint

So, as we drove along I made a few calls and sent a couple of messages and rounded up most of our friends from day one. With Di's kind offer of a lift we would be able to return to our start point outside The Bay Horse at Canal Foot in Ulverston.

Andy and Zoe from Shed 1 Gin had been about to have their tea when I called but dropped everything to come and say hello, Linda from The Bay Horse abandoned her evening rush to come outside for the photos, and Diane thought she was just giving us a quick lift home.

I've often thought that Beth could start a cult. She has a way of roping people into her crazy-ass ideas. Like hauling a beer cask 138 miles around Cumbria ...

As we all stood around chatting and laughing I tried to wrap my head around what we'd just achieved. Eighteen days earlier we'd set out from this very spot with a lot of crazy plans and ideas, and now we were back, all done and dusted with loads of great stories, tons of fabulous memories and, most importantly of all, a whole gaggle of new friends that we'd made along the way. The biggest question now, as everyone kept asking, was 'What's next?' I was far too tired to think about our next ridiculous adventure, but, most pressingly for me 'what's next' was a 6:45am alarm call the next day and work in Manchester. I know that all good things must come to an end, but some things end rather more abruptly than others.

BREWERY: Prince of Wales Brewery, Foxfield

WEBSITE: princeofwalesfoxfield.co.uk

BEERS: Made on site bitter, scrumpy and other beers

TOURS? No

TAP ROOM? The pub is the tap room

STOCKED: Only sell their beers in their pub

Epilogue part I

I'M NOT GONNA LIE to you; the 6:45am alarm call for Manchester was tough. In my 'other life' I deliver training courses, and it was quite entertaining to spend the day with a group of people, many of whom complained that they'd had a tough couple of weeks. I stretched my aching legs and back, noted the marks on my arm from the clegg bites, and bit my tongue.

I had one more treat awaiting me at the end of the day. One more way to eke out our adventure just a little bit longer. Before we set off we'd been to visit The Carlisle Brewing Co., owned and run by Alison and Alain. Our original route plan had taken us right up there; for various reasons the route had had to change, but I didn't want to miss them out, so we had a few of their brews on hand to toast our success.

Alison originates from Carlisle and her husband, Alain, is from the North East. They lived together in Gateshead for many years with Alison working in publishing while Alain was a social worker in a children's home. Work took them to Wales where they lived for ten years before deciding, in the words of Monty Python, that now was time to do something completely different.

I'm not saying they're impulsive but friends of their suggested that they should run a pub, so six months later they bought one – The Spinners Arms in Cummersdale. That was in 2007 and they quickly realised that they had to think creatively to keep a pub alive in a difficult market, which they did. In 2013 they got a grant from DEFRA that allowed them to create their own small brewery behind the pub and their second ever ale won Beer of the Festival at the Solway Beer Festival. Not a bad start, whichever way you look at it.

Alain is in charge of the recipes and brews beers that he enjoys drinking himself – all of them good, traditional, local ales. It was while talking to them that I realised how much authors and brewers have in common (apart from the fact that I spend an inordinate amount of time

working in my PJs) – we both create something we love for other people to consume. In the same way that me and Steve always get excited when we see our books in a bookshop (seriously, that *never* gets old), so Alison and Alain get the giggles whenever they walk into a pub and spot their beer on the pumps. They also create something from nothing, and get a real buzz out of people enjoying their beers.

The Carlisle Brewing Co. is still very local, but you should be able to find their beers across most of Cumbria and up into southern Scotland.

It had been a long couple of weeks and now, finally, I could put my feet up properly and enjoy a pint (or two!) without the worry of either hauling a beer cask or having to get up for a train the next day. I was finally done. Well, it turns out, mostly done ...

BREWERY: Carlisle Brewing Company

WEBSITE: carlislerealale.com

BEERS: Flaxen, Spun Gold, Citadel, Magic Number, Oatmeal Stout, Carlisle Bell, La'al Clarty Jewkle and others

TOURS? Not at present

TAP ROOM? The Spinners Arms, Cummersdale, CA2 6BD

STOCKED: Local pubs and shops

Epilogue part II

JUST A WEEK LATER I was well recovered and beginning to ponder how I'd put the book together. The washing was all done, we both now smelled considerably better than we had a week or so earlier, and our weather-beaten tans were beginning to fade.

Delores, our seventeen-year-old (t)rusty motorhome was in for an MOT in Ings. She failed. Welding was needed so I kept myself amused by going for a walk and discovering another local brewery – this time the Watemill Inn in Ings.

By now I had an affliction which meant that I had to chat to every small brewer I encountered, but it was so much harder explaining the adventure without the cask a proof. I ordered some food and sat in a corner. Pretty soon the head brewer appeared. He was thoroughly charming and explained that it was a family businesses, founded by Alan in 1986 when he returned home to Cumbria after a stint living in Devon.

After Brian retired and passed away, his son Brian took up the brewing reins, but he had sadly passed away a few weeks before my visit. The head brewer was now in charge until Brian's sons, currently too young to run a brewery, decided whether to follow the family tradition. All of their beers are brewed to traditional recipes and they make a range of ales and IPAs. From time to time they experiment with new recipes and flavours, which always get their first airing in The Watermill.

They are also clearly dog nuts, all their beers have funny dog related names, Dog'th Vader, A Winters Tail, a Bit'er Ruff, to name a few.

It really is a rather lovely pub, tucked away off the main road, and certainly worth a visit. They're also very accommodating of worried motorhome owners awaiting MOT results. (She passed in the end, phew!)

At the time of writing I'm thinking how to reunite with Cask #056. We need marketing for the run-up to launch, I'm thinking of taking it up Scafell. In the meantime, you will be able to see him when we go to markets when selling our books or at home in Unsworth's Brewery where he proudly available for photos next to a picture of us all on top of Helvellyn. I'm sure he's missing the adventures but then again, living in the brewery maybe he is given plenty of beer to drink, so is probably quite happy.

Epilogue part III – son of epilogue

The Lockdown Update – Autumn 2020

OBVIOUSLY, WE COMPLETED OUR HIKE in a pre-COVID world and, it's fair to say, that the COVID lockdown of early 2020 had a huge impact on all of the breweries we visited. Throughout the entire period it was amazing to see how all of the small local businesses adapted to the rapidly changing and enormously challenging conditions.

Many places evolved to offer take-away services or home delivery. At the start of lockdown we saw pubs offering beer, which would otherwise have had to be thrown away, free in exchange for a donation to charity. What we also saw was a huge surge in support for all of our local Cumbrian businesses, many of which suffered huge losses due to the pandemic.

I caught up with a couple of folks in the post lockdown chaos to find out how they'd coped, and I thought it would be interesting to share their stories.

Carlisle Brewing Company

'We had a strange lockdown, our pub was obviously closed and, as I write this not yet re-opened, we won't be open for the first weekend as we still have so much to do and get ordered and delivered.

The joy of running a brewery and pub means that we basically have two jobs instead of one, so fully concentrating on one can be tricky. We continued with the brewery, moving into home delivery of beer in a box. We got shed loads of support, which meant we kept brewing, even managing to get two new recipes out there – Sufficient Darkness and Irresponsible Hopping, a nice 5.6% dark one and a 6.0% IPA – it actually gave us the chance to do beers that we can't do that often as the pubs we supply generally want the lower ABV pale ones.

As part of doing this, we passed on a donation to the customer's nominated pub, which meant that over 50 pubs got a little bit of cash and a bit of a boost to show that that their regulars were thinking of them – we also managed to send a lump of cash to the food bank in Carlisle from all those orders that didn't nominate a pub.

So a bit of a mixed bag but on the whole, we've survived – well, at least, we're still here! I'm making my first proper delivery run today, which feels great – I know it will be heads down to get through the next six months and it's sad to think that not everyone will make it through this but we're hoping that the majority of our customers come through as unscathed as possible – we know we've missed the pub!'

The Bay Horse Pub – our start and end point.

'While Bob has been getting a taste of what a very long overdue retirement might be like, thoroughly enjoying himself at our beautiful home high on the hills of Kirkby in Furness, I have discovered I have an eye for photography (literally, as I have a congenital cataract, but discovered the built-in zoom on my camera lets me see things I might have missed).

I've been enjoying myself getting up at the crack of dawn to see the sunrise on the estuary. I see this when it comes up at a decent time most mornings on breakfast shift, but during lockdown have been able to venture up the canal next to the pub, and along the estuary and back to the fields to follow the local wildlife, especially the swans and cygnets and recently a female deer. Some of my photos have even been used by Ulverston BID (Business Improvement District) in local promotional guides.

We also had a teddies' tea party set up in the conservatory to keep local children entertained and the three Polish girls plus one from Nepal who work and live with us, helped deliver homemade scones with jam and cream to all the hamlet of Canal Foot as part of the celebrations we had down here for V.E. Day.

We have also done some maintenance painting around The Bay Horse, and Bob has been busy at home fixing gates and all sorts in his shed, growing lots of vegetables and generally enjoying what he likes doing best, keeping himself busy.

Ok. We have no money coming in, but we have been very happy! We have some lovely customers who we miss but then you remind yourself of the ones you don't and hey ho!'

Epilogue part IV – daughter of epilogue – summer 2021

RATHER LIKE LOCKDOWNS, you never know quite when the epilogues are going to end and, hopefully, this will be the last one.

You don't need us to tell you that 2020/2021 were challenging years but, thankfully, it looks like most of the businesses have made it through intact and, judging by the record numbers of people in the county, they're finally having the bumper year they needed to make up for lost time.

A few updates for places that we visited …

The Prince of Wales in Foxfield is closed at the time of writing. The owners had been planning to sell before we visited them, so we guess COVID was the final push for them to move on. It's a lovely pub in a cracking location, so we really hope someone snaps it up soon and showers it with the love it so richly deserves.

The fabulous New Bookshop in Cockermouth is on the market. They really have been so incredibly supportive of local writers that we sincerely hope the new owners, whoever they may be, follow in their footsteps.

Skiddaw House went on the market too – it turns out a baby has caused the owners to sell up and find something a little less isolated. And maybe with things like electricity and WiFi. Whoever owns it in the future, it will still be an incredible place to visit, and the memory of Debs and Andy, and that glorious night's sleep, will never leave us.

We hope you enjoyed the book and, the next time you visit Cumbria, please support our amazing local pubs and breweries; I know they will be delighted to see you.